Volume 1A Topics 1–4

Authors

Randall I. Charles
Professor Emeritus
Department of Mathematics
San Jose State University
San Jose, California

Jennifer Bay-Williams
Professor of Mathematics Education
College of Education and Human
Development
University of Louisville
Louisville, Kentucky

Robert Q. Berry, III
Associate Professor of
Mathematics Education
Department of Curriculum,
Instruction and Special Education
University of Virginia
Charlottesville, Virginia

Janet H. Caldwell
Professor of Mathematics
Rowan University
Glassboro, New Jersey

Zachary Champagne
Assistant in Research
Florida Center for Research in Science,
Technology, Engineering, and
Mathematics (FCR-STEM)
Jacksonville, Florida

Juanita Copley
Professor Emerita, College of Education
University of Houston
Houston, Texas

Warren Crown
Professor Emeritus of Mathematics
Education
Graduate School of Education
Rutgers University
New Brunswick, New Jersey

Francis (Skip) Fennell
L. Stanley Bowlsbey Professor
of Education and Graduate and
Professional Studies
McDaniel College
Westminster, Maryland

Karen Karp
Professor of Mathematics Education
Department of Early Childhood and
Elementary Education
University of Louisville
Louisville, Kentucky

Stuart J. Murphy
Visual Learning Specialist
Boston, Massachusetts

Jane F. Schielack
Professor of Mathematics
Associate Dean for Assessment and
Pre K–12 Education, College of Science
Texas A&M University
College Station, Texas

Jennifer M. Suh
Associate Professor for
Mathematics Education
George Mason University
Fairfax, Virginia

Jonathan A. Wray
Mathematics Instructional Facilitator
Howard County Public Schools
Ellicott City, Maryland

SAVVAS
LEARNING COMPANY

Mathematicians

Roger Howe
Professor of Mathematics
Yale University
New Haven, Connecticut

Gary Lippman
Professor of Mathematics and
Computer Science
California State University, East Bay
Hayward, California

ELL Consultants

Janice R. Corona
Independent Education Consultant
Dallas, Texas

Jim Cummins
Professor
The University of Toronto
Toronto, Canada

Debbie Crisco
Math Coach
Beebe Public Schools
Beebe, Arkansas

Kathleen A. Cuff
Teacher
Kings Park Central School District
Kings Park, New York

Erika Doyle
Math and Science Coordinator
Richland School District
Richland, Washington

Reviewers

Susan Jarvis
Math and Science Curriculum Coordinator
Ocean Springs Schools
Ocean Springs, Mississippi

SAVVAS
LEARNING COMPANY

ISBN-13: 978-0-328-93058-6
ISBN-10:   0-328-93058-X
5 2020

You'll be using these digital resources throughout the year!

Digital Resources

Go to SavvasRealize.com

MP
Math Practices Animations to play anytime

Glossary
Animated Glossary in English and Spanish

Help
Another Look Homework Video for extra help

ACTIVe-book
Student Edition online for showing your work

Solve
Solve & Share problems plus math tools

Tools
Math Tools to help you understand

Games
Math Games to help you learn

Learn
Visual Learning Animation Plus with animation, interaction, and math tools

Assessment
Quick Check for each lesson

eText
Student Edition online

SAVVAS realize. Everything you need for math anytime, anywhere

Contents

KEY

- ● Numbers: Concepts and Counting
- ● Operations and Algebra
- ● Numbers and Computation
- ● Measurement and Data
- ● Geometry

Digital Resources at SavvasRealize.com

TOPICS

And remember your eText is available at SavvasRealize.com!

SavvasRealize.com

TOPIC 1
Numbers 0 to 5

You can use numbers to show the number of objects.

4

Contents

TOPIC 2
Compare Numbers 0 to 5

There are more tennis balls than footballs when you compare.

TOPIC 3
Numbers 6 to 10

You can use counters to show how many.

TOPIC 4
Compare Numbers 0 to 10

There is a greater number of red fish than purple fish.

SavvasRealize.com

TOPIC 5
Classify and Count Data

The animals are classified into a category of animals with hair and a category of animals without hair.

Hair   NO Hair

TOPIC 6
Understand Addition

You can use addition to show joining groups.

__ and __ is __.

SavvasRealize.com

TOPIC 7
Understand Subtraction

This shows 5 − 2 = 3.

Contents

TOPIC 8
More Addition and Subtraction

You can write equations to show parts of numbers.

$$8 = 2 + 6$$

SavvasRealize.com

Contents

F13

Let's take a look at what's coming up in Volume 2!

You can count objects and write the number to tell how many in all.

eleven

TOPIC 9 in Volume 2
Count Numbers to 20

Contents

The equation tells how many cubes in all.

$$10 + 2 = 12$$

TOPIC 10 in Volume 2
Compose and Decompose Numbers 11 to 19

TOPIC 11 in Volume 2
Count Numbers to 100

You can use part of a hundred chart to count and find patterns.

TOPIC 12 in Volume 2
Identify and Describe Shapes

There are flat and solid objects in our environment. The notebook paper and envelope are flat. The cup and tissue box are solid.

SavvasRealize.com

TOPIC 13 in Volume 2
Analyze, Compare, and Create Shapes

The side of this cube is a square.

TOPIC 14 in Volume 2
Describe and Compare Measurable Attributes

You can compare the sizes of different objects.

Shorter

STEP UP to Grade 1 in Volume 2

These lessons help prepare you for Grade 1.

Problem Solving Handbook

Math practices are ways we think about and do math.

Math practices will help you solve problems.

Problem Solving Handbook

Math Practices

1. Make sense of problems and persevere in solving them.

2. Reason abstractly and quantitatively.

3. Construct viable arguments and critique the reasoning of others.

4. Model with mathematics.

5. Use appropriate tools strategically.

6. Attend to precision.

7. Look for and make use of structure.

8. Look for and express regularity in repeated reasoning.

There are good Thinking Habits for each of these math practices.

1 Make sense of problems and persevere in solving them.

My plan was to count the bees. The last number I counted was the total number of bees.

Good math thinkers know what the problem is about. They have a plan to solve it. They keep trying if they get stuck.

How many bees are there in all? How do you know?

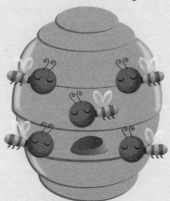

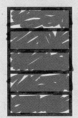

Thinking Habits

What do I need to find?

What do I know?

What's my plan for solving the problem?

What else can I try if I get stuck?

How can I check that my solution make sense?

2 Reason abstractly and quantitatively.

This problem is about the number 4. I can show 4 in a different way to solve the problem.

Good math thinkers know how to think about words and numbers to solve problems.

Daniel sees 4 frogs. He wants to draw 4 dragonflies in a different arrangement. What other way can he show the number 4?

4

4

Thinking Habits

What do the numbers stand for?

How are the numbers in the problem related?

How can I show a word problem using pictures or numbers?

How can I use a word problem to show what an equation means?

Problem Solving Handbook

3 Construct viable arguments and critique the reasoning of others.

Good math thinkers use math to explain why they are right. They talk about math that others do, too.

I used a picture and words to explain my thinking.

How is the second box like the first box?
Explain your answer.

I counted the stars. I counted the counters. Both boxes have 3 things.

Thinking Habits

How can I use math to explain my work?

Am I using numbers and symbols correctly?

Is my explanation clear?

What questions can I ask to understand other people's thinking?

Are there mistakes in other people's thinking?

Can I improve other people's thinking?

4 Model with mathematics.

Good math thinkers use math they know to show and solve problems.

I used the colored boxes to show the correct answer.

Place 2 counters in the nest. Peeps found these worms for her babies. How can you use the model below the nest to show how many worms Peeps found?

Thinking Habits

How can I use the math I know to help solve this problem?

Can I use a drawing, diagram, table, or objects to show the problem?

Can I write an equation to show the problem?

Problem Solving Handbook

5 Use appropriate tools strategically.

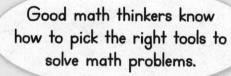
Good math thinkers know how to pick the right tools to solve math problems.

I chose counters to solve the problem.

How many leaves are there in all? Use counters, connecting cubes, or other objects to show how many, and then write the number to tell how many.

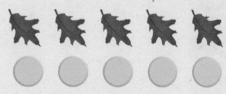

5

Thinking Habits

Which tools can I use?

Is there a different tool I could use?

Am I using the tool correctly?

6 Attend to precision.

Good math thinkers are careful about what they write and say, so their ideas about math are clear.

I was careful when I counted and colored.

Each bird found some worms for her babies. Did they find the same number or different numbers of worms? Color the boxes to show how you know.

Thinking Habits

Am I using numbers, units, and symbols correctly?

Am I using the correct definitions?

Is my answer clear?

Problem Solving Handbook

7 Look for and make use of structure.

Good math thinkers look for patterns in math to help solve problems.

I found a pattern.

How can you tell how many objects you see without counting first?
Explain how you know you are right.

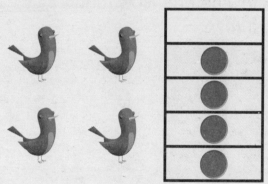

Thinking Habits

Is there a pattern?

How can I describe the pattern?

Can I break the problem into simpler parts?

8 Look for and express regularity in repeated reasoning.

Good math thinkers look for things that repeat in a problem. They use what they learn from one problem to help them solve other problems.

I know that the 1 more repeats. That helped me solve the problem.

The first row has 1 counter colored. Each row has 1 more counter than the row before. How many counters will be in the last row?

Thinking Habits

Does something repeat in the problem?

How can the solution help me solve another problem?

Problem Solving Handbook

Problem Solving Guide

These questions can help you solve problems.

Make Sense of the Problem

Reason
- What do I need to find?
- What given information can I use?
- How are the quantities related?

Think About Similar Problems
- Have I solved problems like this before?

Persevere in Solving the Problem

Model with Math
- How can I use the math I know?
- How can I show the problem?
- Is there a pattern I can use?

Use Appropriate Tools
- What math tools could I use?
- How can I use those tools?

Check the Answer

Make Sense of the Answer
- Is my answer reasonable?

Check for Precision
- Did I check my work?
- Is my answer clear?
- Is my explanation clear?

Some Ways to Show Problems

- Draw a Picture
- Write an Equation

Some Math Tools

- Objects
- Technology
- Paper and Pencil

Problem Solving Recording Sheet

This sheet helps you organize your work.

Name Gretchen

Teaching Tool 1

Problem Solving Recording Sheet

Problem:
5 birds are on a fence.
2 birds fly away.
How many birds are left?

MAKE SENSE OF THE PROBLEM

Need to Find	Given
I need to find how many birds are left.	5 birds are on a fence. 2 birds fly away.

PERSEVERE IN SOLVING THE PROBLEM

Some Ways to Represent Problems
☑ Draw a Picture
☑ Write an Equation

Some Math Tools
☐ Objects
☐ Technology
☑ Paper and Pencil

Solution and Answer

3 birds
5 – 2 = 3

CHECK THE ANSWER

I listened to the problem again. I checked my picture and counted the birds that were left, 3 birds. My answer is correct.

TT1

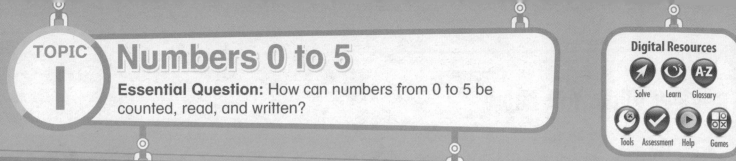

TOPIC 1 — Numbers 0 to 5

Essential Question: How can numbers from 0 to 5 be counted, read, and written?

Digital Resources

Solve Learn Glossary

Tools Assessment Help Games

Rain

It rains on some days. It is sunny on other days.

Math and Science Project: Weather Changes

Directions Read the character speech bubbles to students. **Find Out!** Have students pay attention to the daily weather changes. Say: *The weather changes from day to day. Talk to friends and relatives about the weather. Ask them to help you record the number of sunny days and rainy days from Monday to Friday.* **Journal: Make a Poster** Have students make a poster of the weather information they collected. Have them draw suns for the number of sunny days and clouds with raindrops for the number of rainy days. Then have students write the numbers to tell how many.

Name _____

Review What You Know

1

2

3

4

5

6

Directions Have students: **1** draw a circle around the animal that is on the right; **2** draw a circle around the animal that is on the left; **3** draw a circle around the animal that is green; **4–6** draw a line from each object in the top row to an object in the bottom row.

My Word Cards

Directions Have students cut out the vocabulary cards. Read the front of the card, and then ask them to explain what the word or phrase means.

A-Z Glossary

count	one	two
three	number	four

My Word Cards

Directions Review the definitions and have students study the cards. Extend learning by having students draw pictures for each word on a separate piece of paper.

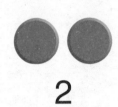

2

Point to the group of counters.
Say: *There are* **two** *counters.*

1

Point to the counter.
Say: *There is* **one** *counter.*

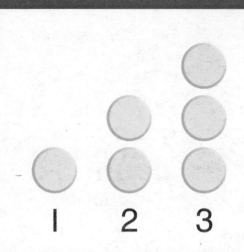

1 2 3

Point to each column of counters.
Say: *When I* **count**, *I say 1, 2, 3 . . .*

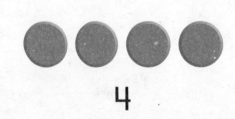

4

Point to the group of counters.
Say: *There are* **four** *counters.*

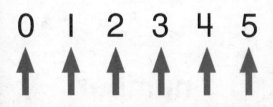

0 1 2 3 4 5

Point to each arrow.
Say: *Each arrow points to a* **number**.

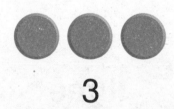

3

Point to the group of counters.
Say: *There are* **three** *counters.*

My Word Cards

A-Z
Glossary

five	**zero**	**none**
whole	**part**	**order**

My Word Cards

0

Point to the 0.
Say: *Another word for 0 is* **none**.

0

Point to the 0.
Say: *This number is* **zero**.

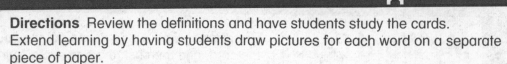

5

Point to the group of counters.
Say: *There are* **five** *counters.*

0→1→2→3→4→5

Point to the picture.
Say: *These numbers are in* **order** *from 0 to 5.*

Point to the bananas in the circle.
Say: *The 3 bananas are* **part** *of this group of 5 fruits.*

Point to the group of fruits.
Say: *The group of 5 fruits is the* **whole** *group.*

Directions Have students place 2 counters in the nest on the workmat. Say: *Peeps the bird found these worms for her babies. Draw a circle around the colored box that shows how many worms Peeps found. Tell how you know you are correct.*

I can ... count 1, 2, and 3 objects.

I can also model with math.

Topic 1 | Lesson 1

Digital Resources at SavvasRealize.com

seven

☆ Guided Practice

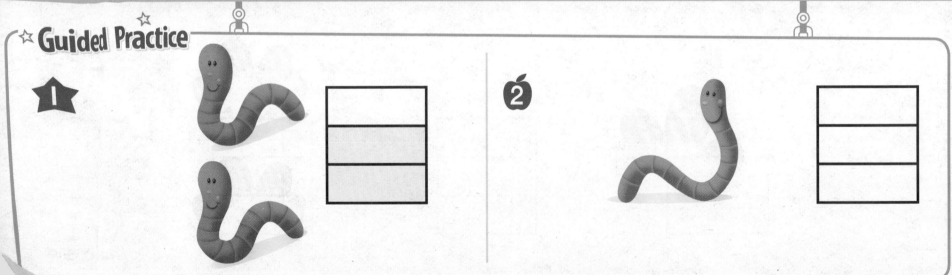

⭐ **1**

2

ions ⭐ and ❷ Have students color a box as they count each worm to show how many.

ight

Topic I | Lesson I

3

4

5

Directions **3** and **4** Have students color a box as they count each worm to show how many. **Vocabulary** Have students **count** the worms, and color a box as they count each worm aloud.

Topic 1 | Lesson 1

nine

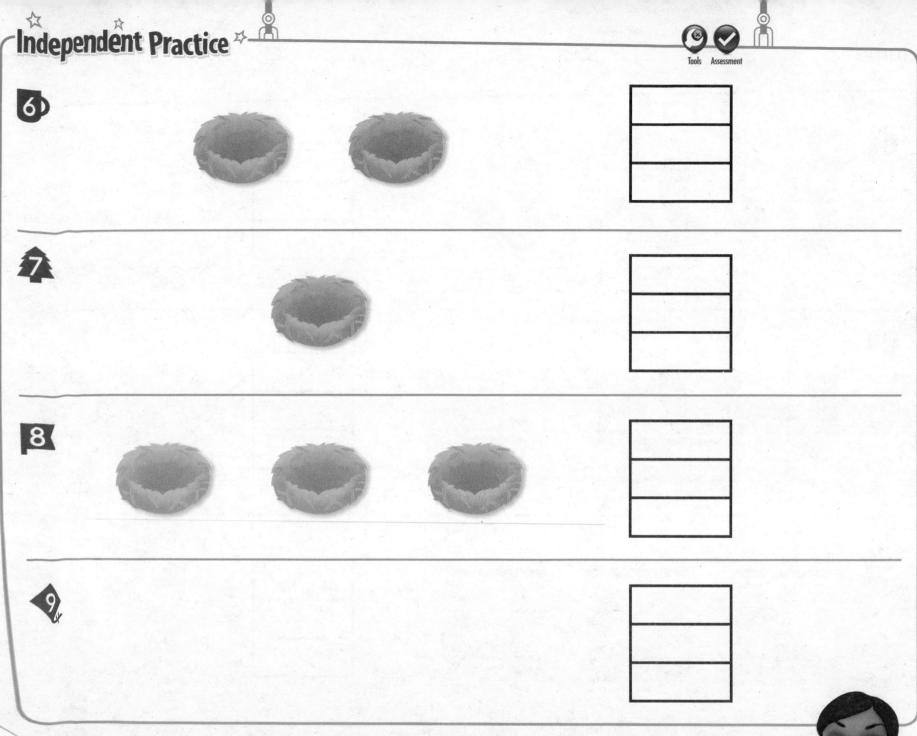

6 🍵

7 🌲

8 🚩

9 🔶

Directions **6–8** Have students color a box as they count each nest to show how many. **9 Higher Order Thinking** Have students draw 1, 2, or 3 nests, and then color a box as they draw each nest to show how many.

Name _____

Help   Tools   Games

Another Look!

HOME ACTIVITY Have your child count groups of 1, 2, and 3 objects.

 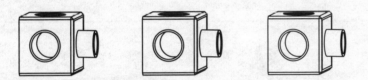

 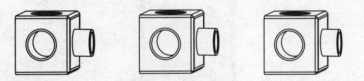

Directions Say: *Use connecting cubes or other objects to model making 2, and then color a cube for each cube you count.* Give students 3 cubes or other small counting objects. Have students: ⭐ choose 2 cubes or objects, and then color a cube as they count each cube to show how many; 🍎 choose 1 cube or object, and then color a cube as they count each cube to show how many; 🐦 choose 3 cubes or objects, and then color a cube as they count each cube to show how many.

4

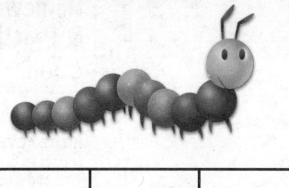

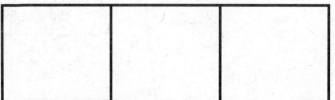

5

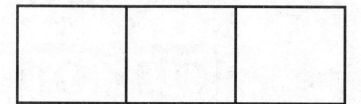

6

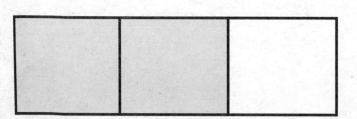

7

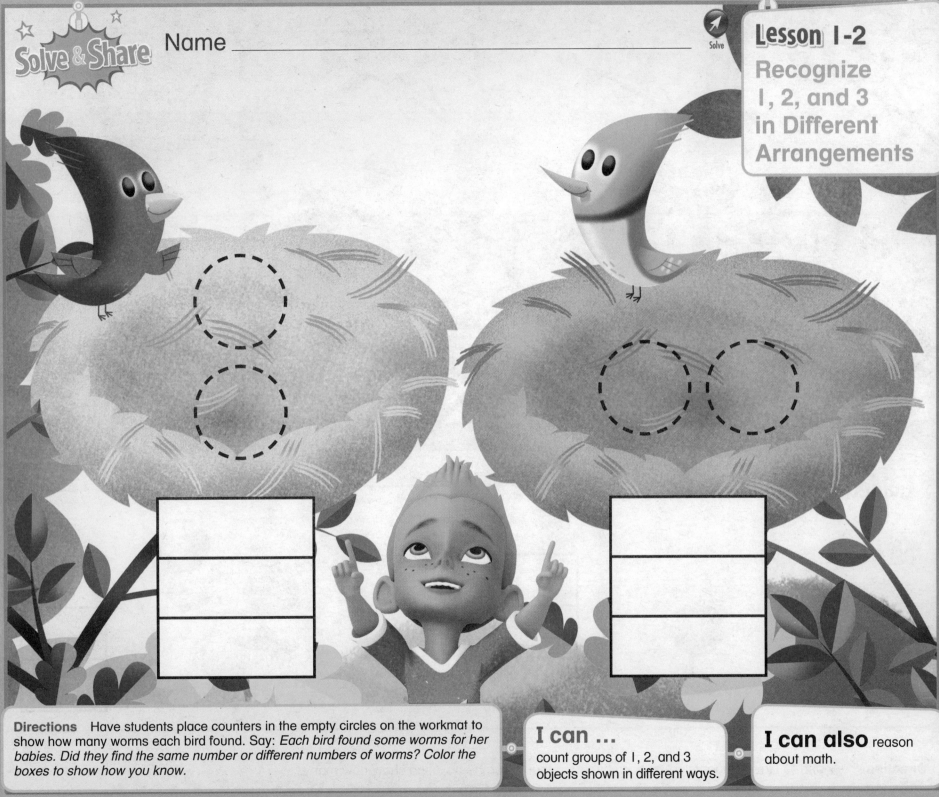

Directions Have students place counters in the empty circles on the workmat to show how many worms each bird found. Say: *Each bird found some worms for her babies. Did they find the same number or different numbers of worms? Color the boxes to show how you know.*

I can ...
count groups of 1, 2, and 3 objects shown in different ways.

I can also reason about math.

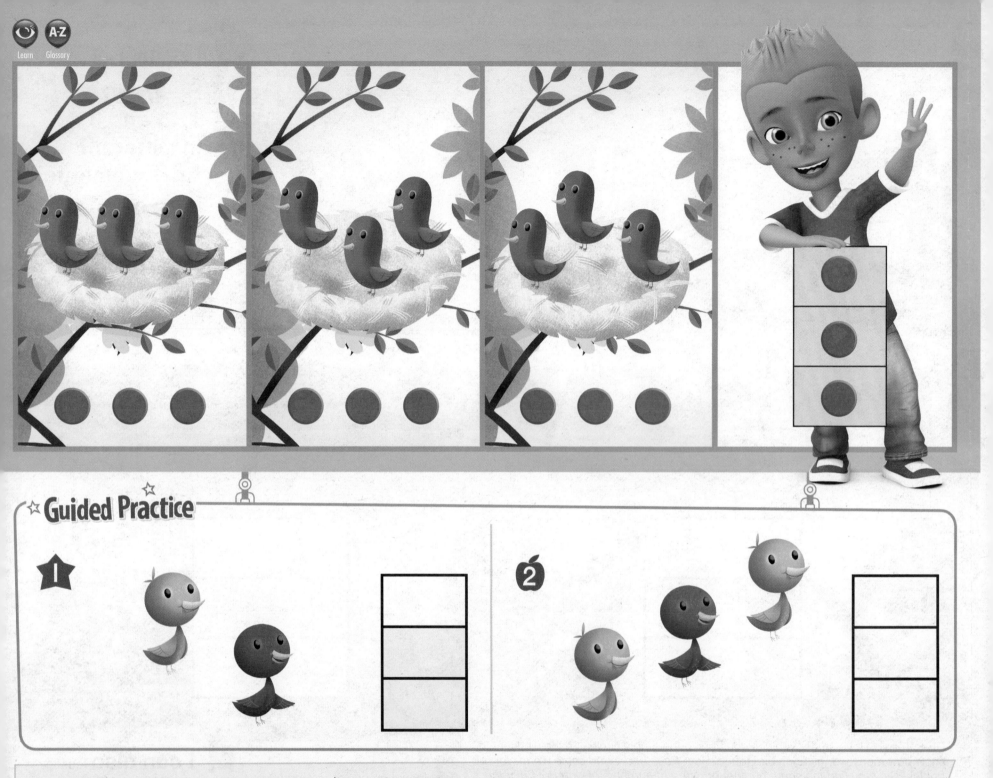

☆ Guided Practice

1

2

Directions ⭐ and ❷ Have students count each bird, and then color the boxes to show how many.

Topic 1 | Lesson 2

Name _____

3 🐦🐦🐦

4 🐦🐦

5 🐦

6 🐦🐦🐦

7 🐦

8 🐦🐦

Directions **3**–**8** Have students count each bird, and then color the boxes to show how many.

Topic 1 | Lesson 2

fifteen **15**

Independent Practice

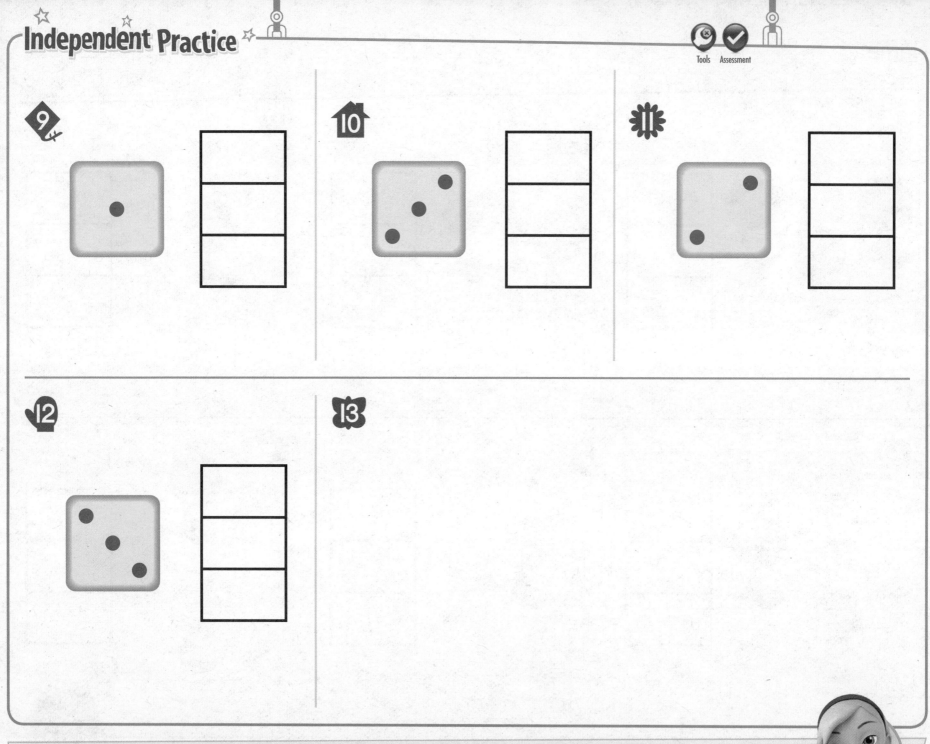

★ 9

🏠 10

✳ 11

🧤 12

🦋 13

16 sixteen   Copyright © Savvas Learning Company LLC. All Rights Reserved.   **Topic 1** | Lesson 2

Name _____

Another Look!

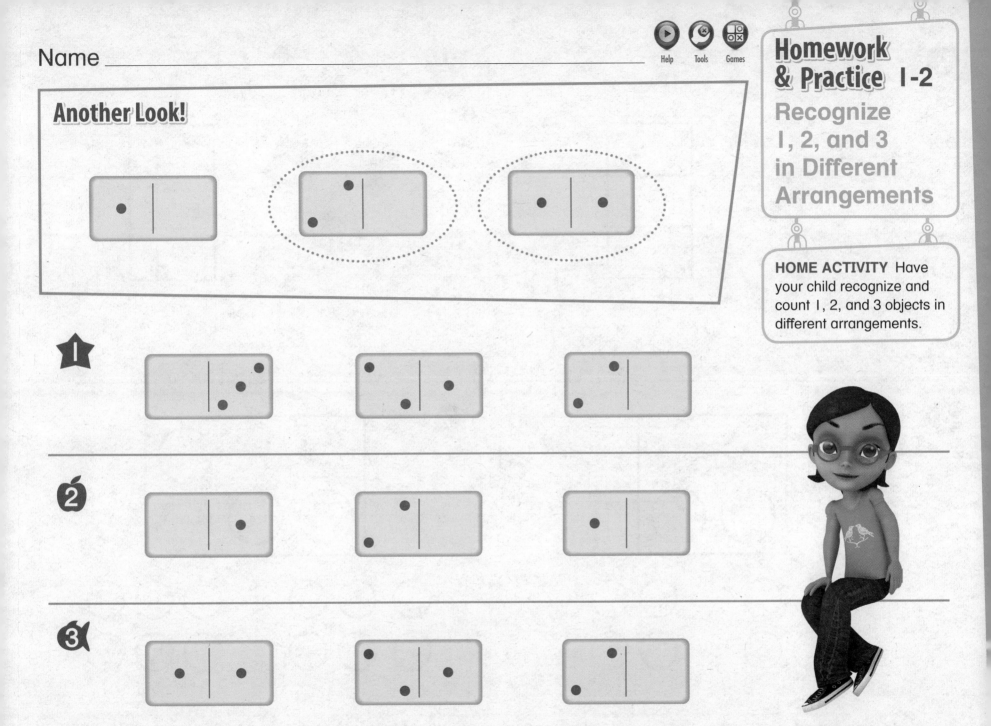

HOME ACTIVITY Have your child recognize and count 1, 2, and 3 objects in different arrangements.

⭐1

②

③

Directions Say: *Count the dots on each dot tile, and then draw a circle around the dot tiles with 2 dots.* Have students: ⭐ draw a circle around the dot tiles with 3 dots; ② draw a circle around the dot tiles with 1 dot; ③ draw a circle around the dot tiles with 2 dots.

Topic 1 | Lesson 2   Digital Resources at SavvasRealize.com   seventeen **17**

4

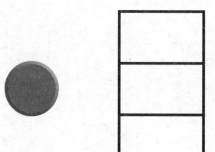

 5

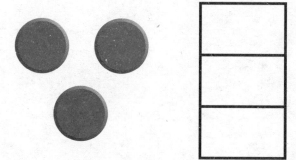

 6

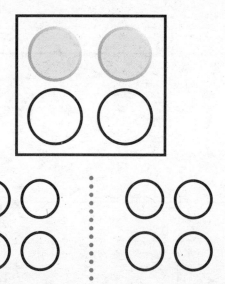

7

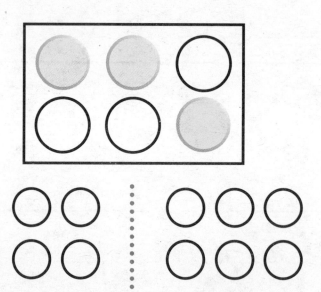

18 eighteen

Topic I | Lesson 2

Solve & Share

Name _____

Solve

Lesson 1-3
Read and Write
1, 2, and 3

Directions Have students place 2 counters in the large cloud on the left side of the workmat. Say: *Alex sees 2 stars in the sky. He draws 2 stars in a cloud. How can he show how many stars in another way? Draw the other way in the small, empty cloud.*

I can ...
read and write the numbers 1, 2, and 3.

I can also reason about math.

3

3

three

☆ Guided Practice

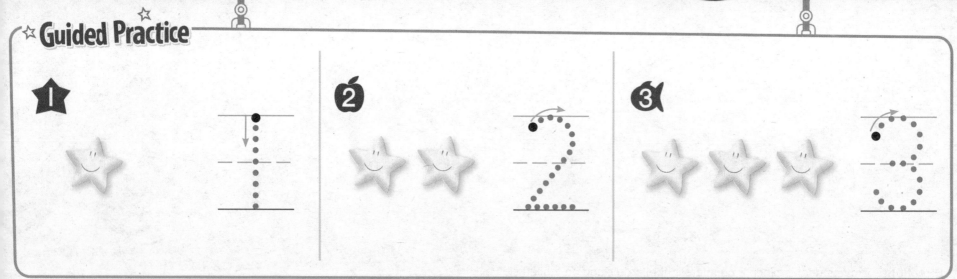

Directions ⭐–❸ Have students count the stars, and then write the number to tell how many.

Topic I | Lesson 3

Name _____

♥ 4

5 ✋

6 ☕

7 🌲

Directions 4—7 Have students count the objects, and then practice writing the number that tells how many.

Topic 1 | Lesson 3

twenty-one **21**

Independent Practice

8

9

10

✳

Directions 8–10 Have students count the objects, and then practice writing the number that tells how many. ✳ **Higher Order Thinking** Have students draw 1, 2, or 3 stars, and then practice writing the number that tells how many.

Topic 1 | Lesson 3

Name _____

Another Look!

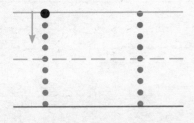 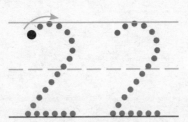 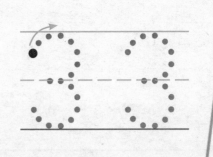

HOME ACTIVITY Draw groups of 1, 2, and 3 circles on 3 index cards. Have your child write the correct number on the back of each card. Then use the cards to practice counting and reading the numbers 1, 2, and 3.

_____

- - - - - - - - - - - - - -

_____

Directions Say: *Practice writing the numbers 1, 2, and 3.* Then have students: ⭐ count the moons, and then write the number of moons under each picture; 🍎 count the stars, and then write the number of stars under each picture.

3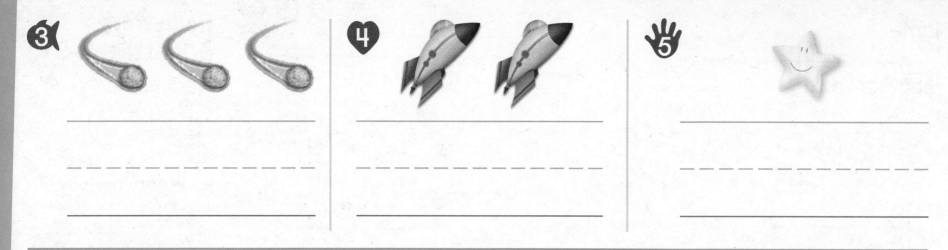

_____

- - - - - - - - - - -

_____

4

_____

- - - - - - - - - - -

_____

5

_____

- - - - - - - - - - -

_____

6

2

_____

7

_____

- - - - - - - - - - -

_____

Directions **3**–**5** Have students count the objects, and then practice writing the number that tells how many.
6 **Higher Order Thinking** Have students look at the number, and then draw moons to show how many.
7 **Higher Order Thinking** Have students draw 1, 2, or 3 rockets, and then practice writing the number that tells how many.

Name _____

I can ...
count 4 and 5 objects.

I can also model with math.

☆ Guided Practice

1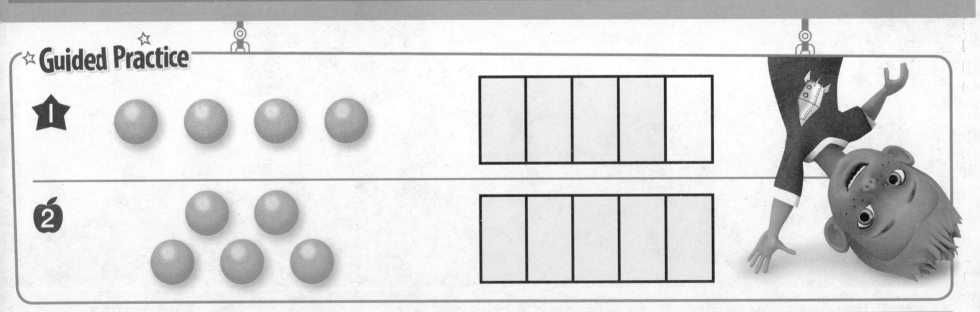

2

Directions 🟊 and 🍎 Have students color a box as they count each orange to show how many.

Name _____

3

4

5

6

Directions **3–6** Have students color a box as they count each piece of fruit to show how many.

Topic I | Lesson 4   twenty-seven **27**

Independent Practice

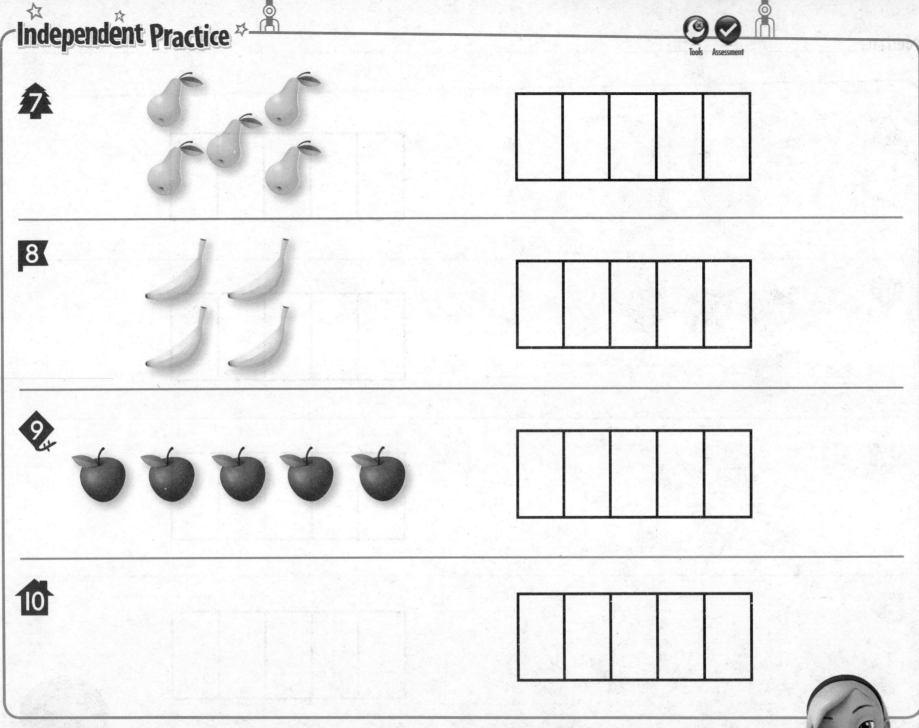

7

8

9

10

Directions **7–9** Have students color a box as they count each piece of fruit to show how many. **10** **Higher Order Thinking** Have students draw 4 or 5 oranges, and then color a box as they draw each orange to show how many.

28 twenty-eight

Copyright © Savvas Learning Company LLC. All Rights Reserved.

Topic I | Lesson 4

Name _____

Help Tools Games

Another Look!

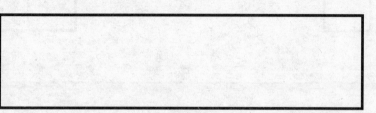

HOME ACTIVITY Have your child count groups of 4 objects. Then have him or her draw pictures of 4 objects. Repeat using the number 5.

Directions Say: *Count the dots in the blue box. Draw a counter for each dot you count.* – Have students draw a counter for each dot they count, and then use counters or objects to show that number.

4

5

6

7

Directions ♥ and ✋ Have students color a box as they count each flower to show how many. ☕ **Higher Order Thinking** Have students color red each group of 4 objects the clowns have and color yellow each group of 5 objects the clowns have. 🌲 **Higher Order Thinking** Have students draw 4 or 5 flowers, and then color a box as they draw each flower to show how many.

30 thirty

Topic I | Lesson 4

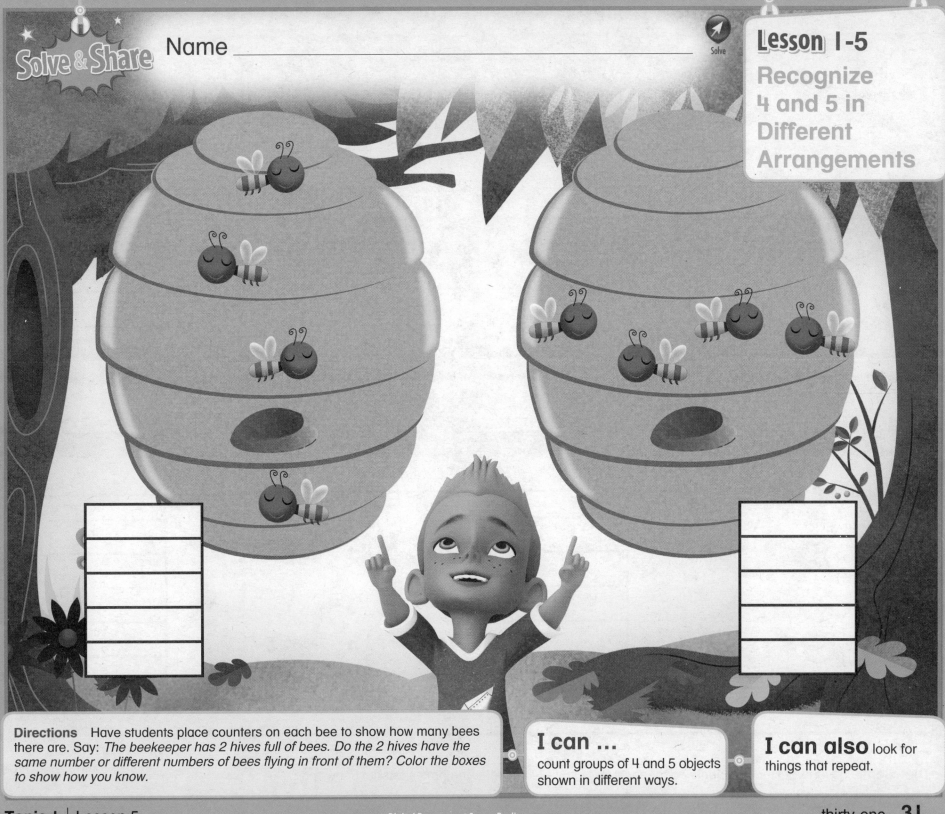

Directions Have students place counters on each bee to show how many bees there are. Say: *The beekeeper has 2 hives full of bees. Do the 2 hives have the same number or different numbers of bees flying in front of them? Color the boxes to show how you know.*

I can ... count groups of 4 and 5 objects shown in different ways.

I can also look for things that repeat.

☆ Guided Practice

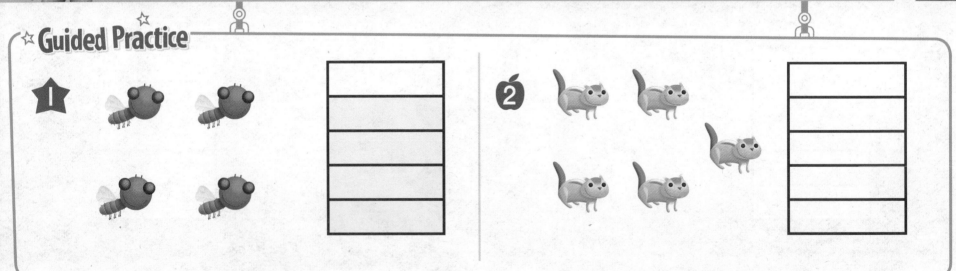

1

2

Directions 🌟 and 🍎 Have students count each animal, and then color the boxes to show how many.

3

4

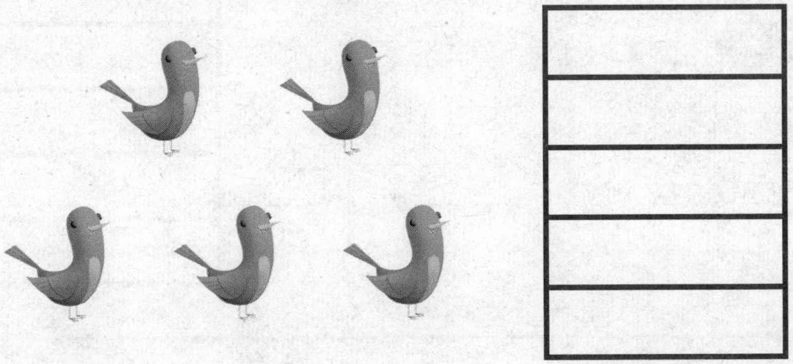

5

6

7

8

Directions ❸–❽ Have students count the birds, and then color the boxes to show how many.

Independent Practice

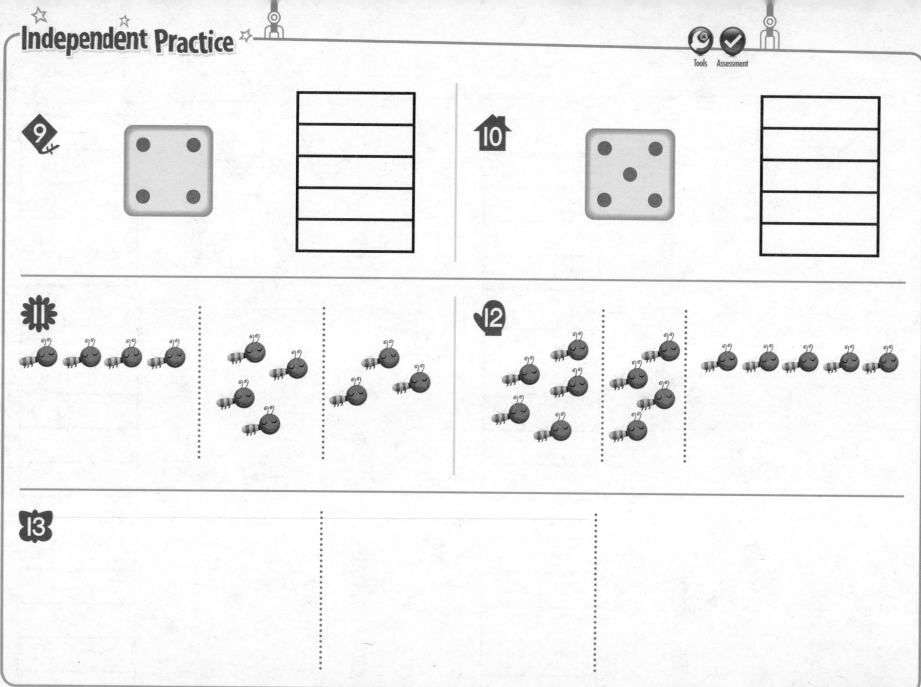

Directions Have students: ✿ and 🏠 count the dots, and then color the boxes to show how many; ✷ count the groups, and then draw a circle around the groups that show 4; 🧤 count the groups, and then draw a circle around the groups that show 5. 🔢 **Higher Order Thinking** Have students draw 5 counters in the first space, and then draw 5 counters in two different ways in the other two spaces.

Topic 1 | Lesson 5

Name _____

Help   Tools   Games

Homework & Practice 1-5

Recognize 4 and 5 in Different Arrangements

Another Look!

 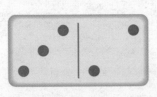 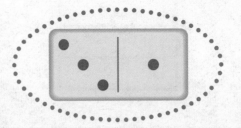

HOME ACTIVITY Have your child recognize and count 4 and 5 objects in different arrangements.

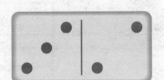  

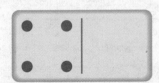  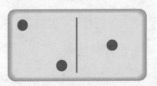

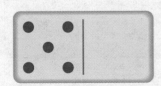 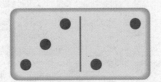 

Directions Say: *Count the dots on each dot tile, and then draw a circle around the dot tiles with 4 dots.* Then have students: ⭐ draw a circle around the dot tiles with 5 dots; ❷ draw a circle around the dot tiles with 4 dots; ❸ draw a circle around the dot tiles with 5 dots.

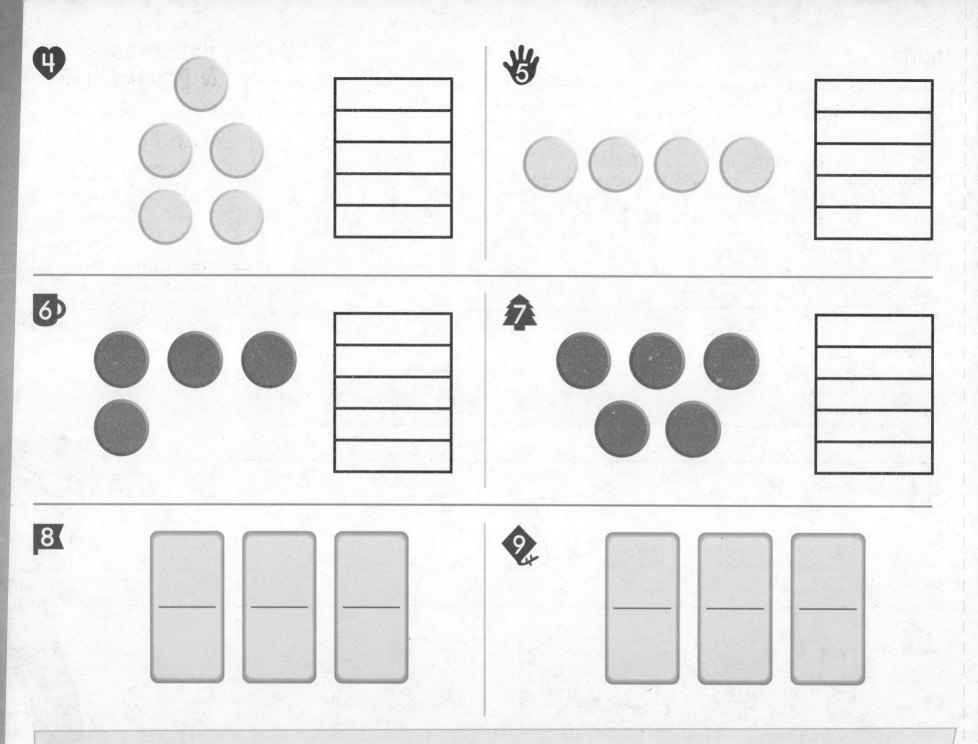

Directions 4—7 Have students count the counters, and then color the boxes to show how many. **8 Higher Order Thinking** Have students draw 4 dots on each dot tile to show three different dot tiles. **9 Higher Order Thinking** Have students draw 5 dots on each dot tile to show three different dot tiles.

Name _____

Solve

Solve & Share

Directions Have students place 5 counters on the lily pad on the left side of the workmat. Say: *Alex sees 5 frogs on the lily pad. He glues pictures of 5 frogs on one lily pad. How can he show how many frogs in another way? Draw the other way on the empty lily pad.*

I can ...
read and write the numbers 4 and 5.

I can also reason about math.

4

4

four

☆ Guided Practice

1

2

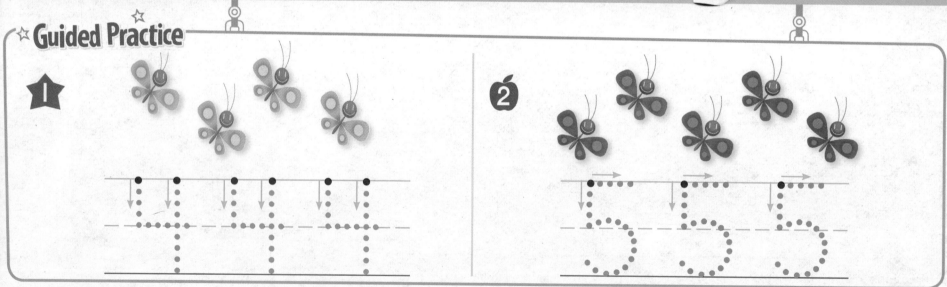

Directions 1 and 2 Have students count the butterflies, and then practice writing the number that tells how many.

Name _____

3 ● ● ● ● ● ●

- - - - - - - - - -

_____

4 ● ● ●

- - - - - - - - - -

_____

5

- - - - - - - - - -

_____

6

- - - - - - - - - -

_____

Directions ❸—❻ Have students count the frogs, and then practice writing the number that tells how many.

Topic 1 | Lesson 6   thirty-nine **39**

Independent Practice

7

_____

- - - - - - - - - - - - - - -

_____

8

_____

- - - - - - - - - - - - - - -

_____

9

_____

- - - - -

_____

Directions **7** and **8** Have students count the dragonflies, and then practice writing the number that tells how many.
9 Higher Order Thinking Have students count the blue birds and the yellow birds, color a box for each bird, and then write the numbers to tell how many.

     Topic 1 | Lesson 6

Name _____

Another Look!

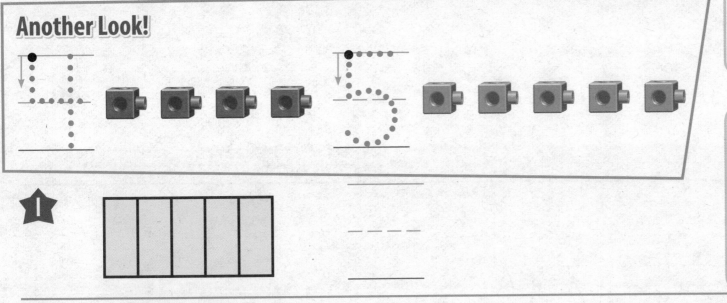

1 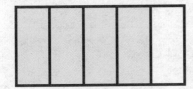 _____

2 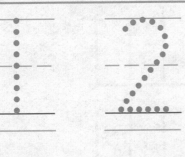 _____

3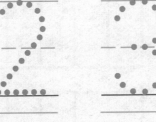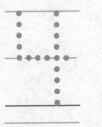

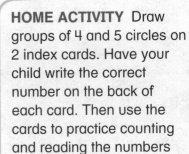

Directions Say: *Count the cubes, and then write the numbers to tell how many.* Have students: **1** and **2** count the colored boxes, and then write the number to tell how many; **3** write each number from 1 to 5, and then write each number again.

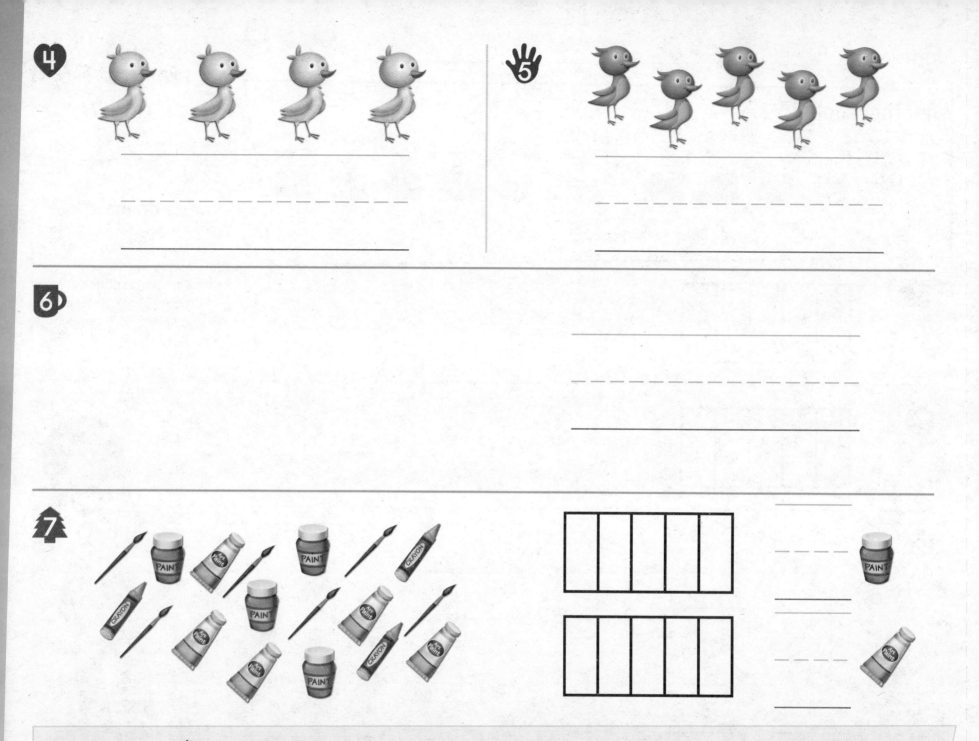

Directions ❤ and ✋ Have students count the number of birds, and then practice writing the number that tells how many. ☕ **Higher Order Thinking** Have students draw 4 or 5 objects, and then practice writing the number that tells how many. 🌲 **Higher Order Thinking** Have students count the bottles of paint and the tubes of paint, color a box for each and then write the numbers to tell how many.

Topic I | Lesson 6

Solve & Share

Directions Have students place 0 counters in the basket on the workmat. Say: *Alex is in a vegetable garden. He does not see any potatoes in the basket. The basket is empty. How can Alex color the boxes to show that there are no potatoes in the basket?*

I can ... use zero to tell when there are no objects.

I can also make math arguments.

Digital Resources at SavvasRealize.com

☆ Guided Practice

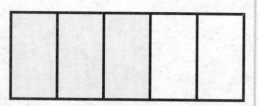

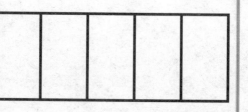

Directions ⭐ and ② Have students color a box as they count each apple to show how many.

Topic 1 | Lesson 7

Name _____

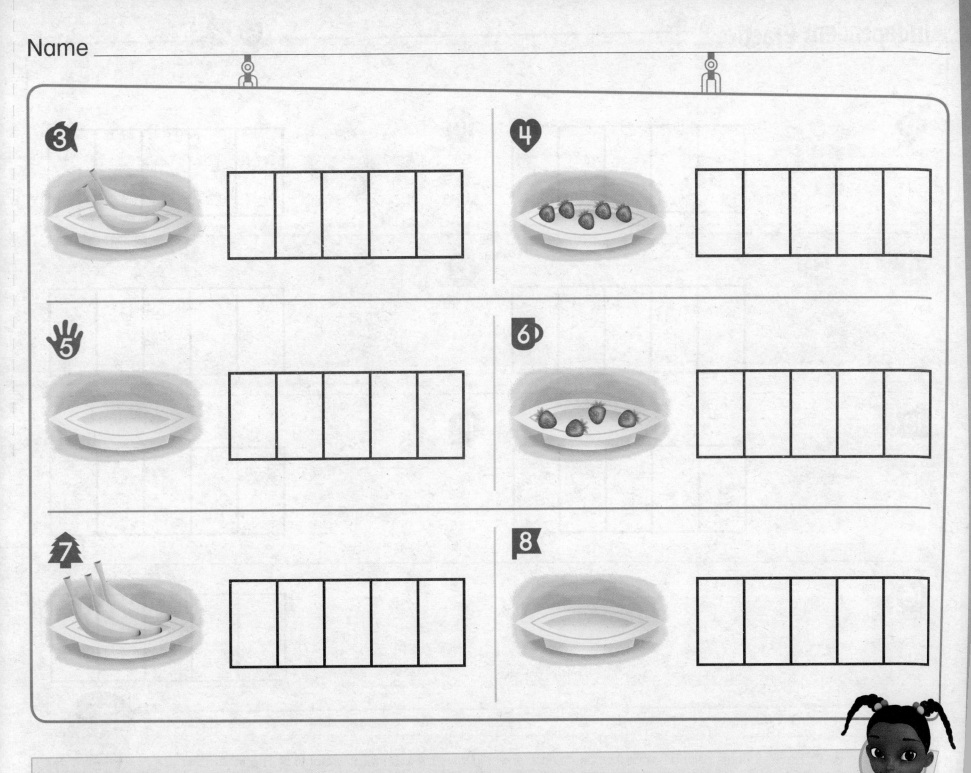

Directions ❸–❽ Have students color a box as they count each piece of fruit to show how many.

Topic 1 | Lesson 7

forty-five **45**

Independent Practice

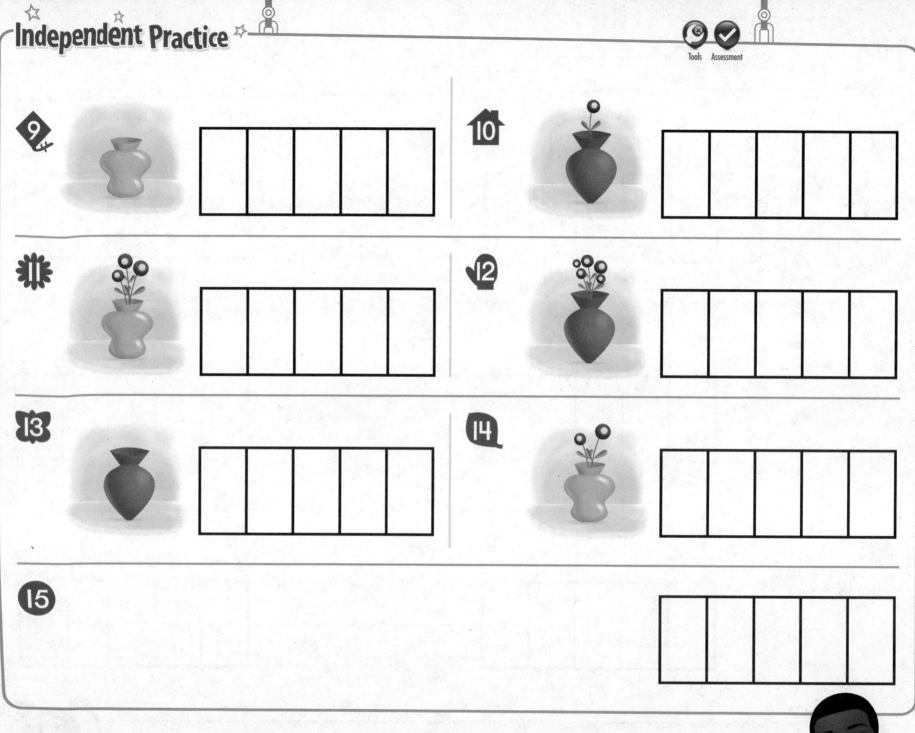

9

10

11

12

13

14

15

46 forty-six

Topic 1 | Lesson 7

Name _____

Another Look!

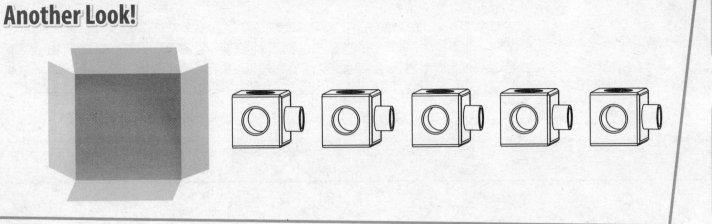

HOME ACTIVITY
Alternate putting objects on a plate and leaving it empty. Have your child identify when there are 0 objects on the plate.

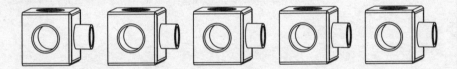

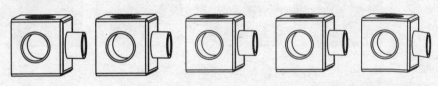

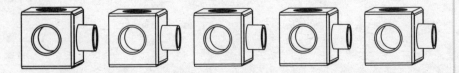

Directions Say: *How many toys are in the box? Use cubes or other objects to show 0, and then color 0 cubes.* Give students 5 cubes or 5 other objects. Have students: ⭐ choose 0 cubes or objects, and then color a cube as they count each cube to show how many; 🍎 choose 2 cubes or objects, and then color a cube as they count each cube to show how many; 🪁 choose 1 cube or object, and then color a cube as they count each cube to show how many; ❤ choose 4 cubes or objects, and then color a cube as they count each cube to show how many.

Directions ✋ Have students color a cube as they count each pear in the bowl to show how many. **6 Higher Order Thinking** Have students draw an apple as they count each cube that shows how many. **7 Higher Order Thinking** Have students draw a plate with some oranges on it, and then draw another plate with 0 oranges on it.

forty-eight

Solve & Share

Name _____

Solve

Directions Say: Alex needs pencils and crayons to do his work. Alex does not see any crayons. How can he show how many pencils and crayons he has? Explain your answer.

I can ... read and write the number 0.

I can also be precise in my work.

zero

⭐ Guided Practice

1

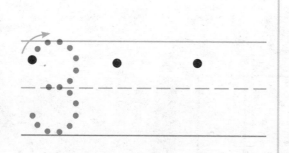

2

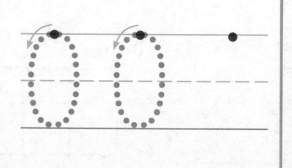

Directions 🟊 and ❷ Have students count the pencils in each pencil holder, and then practice writing the number that tells how many.

Topic I | Lesson 8

Name _____

3 🐟

4 ❤️

5 ✋

6 ☕

7 🌲

8 🚩

Directions ❸–❽ Have students count the pencils in each pencil holder, and then practice writing the number that tells how many.

Independent Practice

9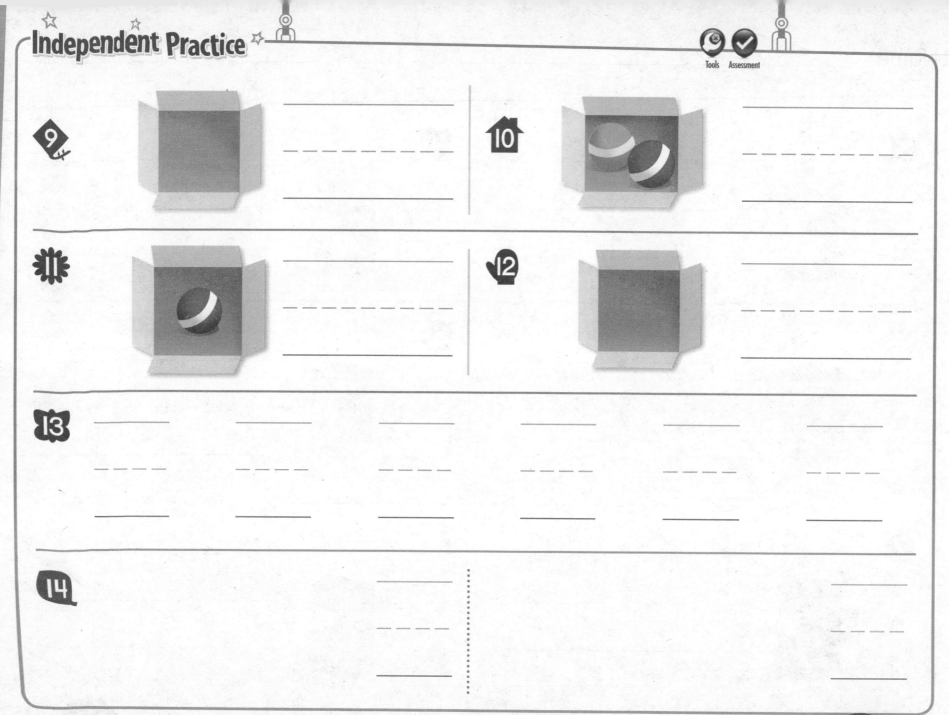

10

11

12

13

14

Directions Have students: **9–12** count the balls in each box, and then practice writing the number that tells how many; **13** practice writing the numbers 0 to 5. **14** **Higher Order Thinking** Have students draw zero counters and write the number to tell how many, and then draw 1 to 5 counters and write the number to tell how many.

fifty-two

Topic 1 | Lesson 8

Name _____

Another Look!

HOME ACTIVITY Have your child show how to read and write the number 0. Have your child use a bowl to model the number 0.

⭐1 _____

2️⃣ _____

3️⃣   4️⃣

5️⃣   6️⃣

Directions Say: *Practice writing the number 0.* Have students: ⭐1 and 2️⃣ count the colored boxes, and then practice writing the number that tells how many; 3️⃣ and 4️⃣ count the trucks in the box, and then write the number to tell how many; 5️⃣ and 6️⃣ count the counters in the hand, and then write the number to tell how many.

7 _____

_ _ _ _ _ _ _

_____

8 _____

_ _ _ _ _ _ _

_____

9 _____

_ _ _ _ _ _ _

_____

10

_____

_ _ _ _ _ _ _ _ _ _ _ _ _

_____

Topic 1 | Lesson 8

Solve

Lesson 1-9
Ways to
Make 5

Directions Say: *5 daisies are planted in a flowerpot. Some are yellow. Some are red. Use counters to show one way to make 5 daisies. Color the daisies yellow and red to show your work. Has the total number of counters changed? Why or why not?*

I can ...
show ways to make 5.

I can also look for patterns.

Digital Resources at SavvasRealize.com

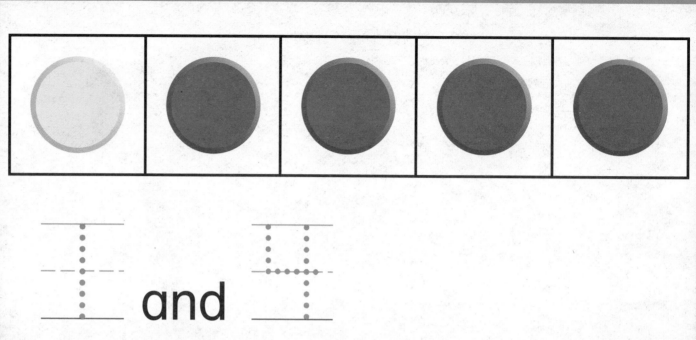

1 and 4

Guided Practice

1

2 and 3

Directions ⭐ Have students use counters to find a way to make 5, color the daisies to show the way, and then write the numbers to tell how many yellow and how many red daisies.

Name _____

2

🌼 🌼 🌼 🌼 🌼

_____ _____

_____ and _____

3

🌹 🌹 🌹 🌹 🌹

_____ _____

_____ and _____

Directions **2** and **3** Have students use counters to find two more ways to make 5, color the flowers yellow and red to show the ways, and then write the numbers to tell how many yellow and how many red flowers.

Topic I | Lesson 9   fifty-seven **57**

Independent Practice

 4

_____ _____

_____ _____

_____ and _____

 5

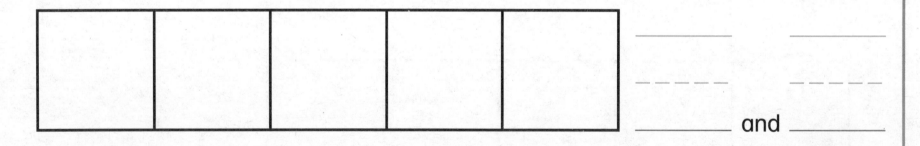

_____ _____

_____ _____

_____ and _____

Directions 🟣 Have students color the flowers yellow and red to show two different ways to make 5, and then write the numbers to tell how many yellow and how many red flowers. 🖐 **Higher Order Thinking** Have students draw a way to make 5 with flowers, and then write the numbers to tell the way to make 5. If needed, have them use counters.

Topic I | Lesson 9

Name _____

Another Look!

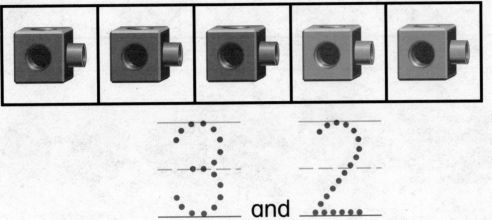

3 and 2

HOME ACTIVITY Have your child show different ways to make 4 in two parts using 4 cards or pictures. Have your child show one part of the 4 cards or pictures facedown and another part faceup. Repeat using the number 5.

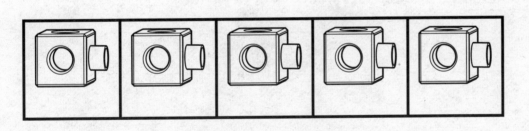

_____ and _____

Directions Say: *Use red and blue cubes or pieces of paper to model a way to make 5, color the cubes to show the way, and then write the numbers to tell how many red and blue cubes.* ⭐ Have students color the cubes red and blue to show a different way to make 5, and then write the numbers to tell how many.

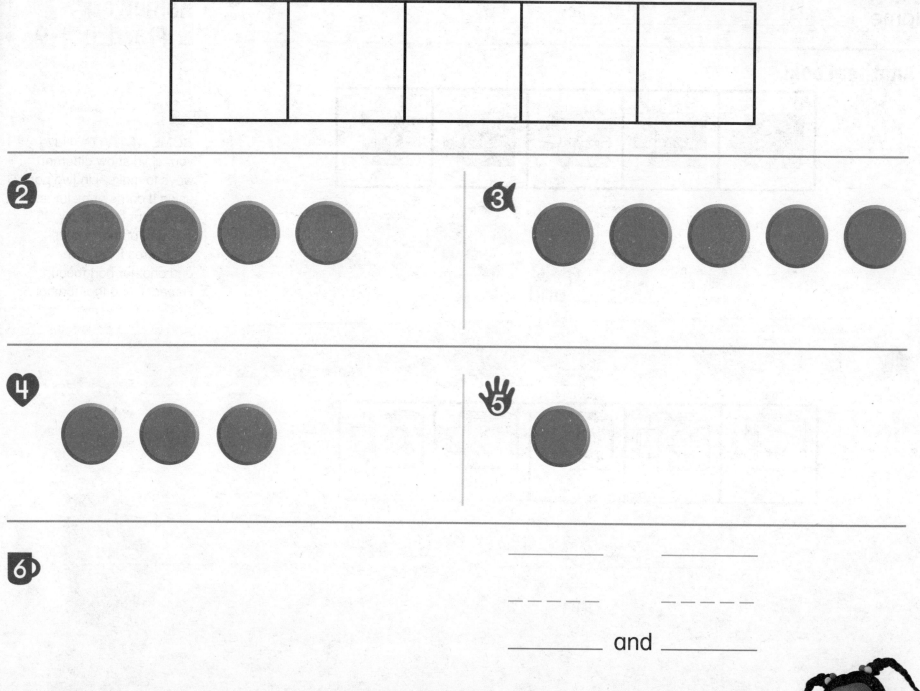

2

3

4

5

6

_____   _____

_ _ _ _ _   _ _ _ _ _

_____ and _____

Directions **2**–**5** Have students use the five-frame above, and then draw yellow counters to complete the ways to make 5.
6 **Higher Order Thinking** Have students draw a way to make 5 with flowers, and then write the numbers to tell how many.

60 sixty

Topic 1 | Lesson 9

Name _____

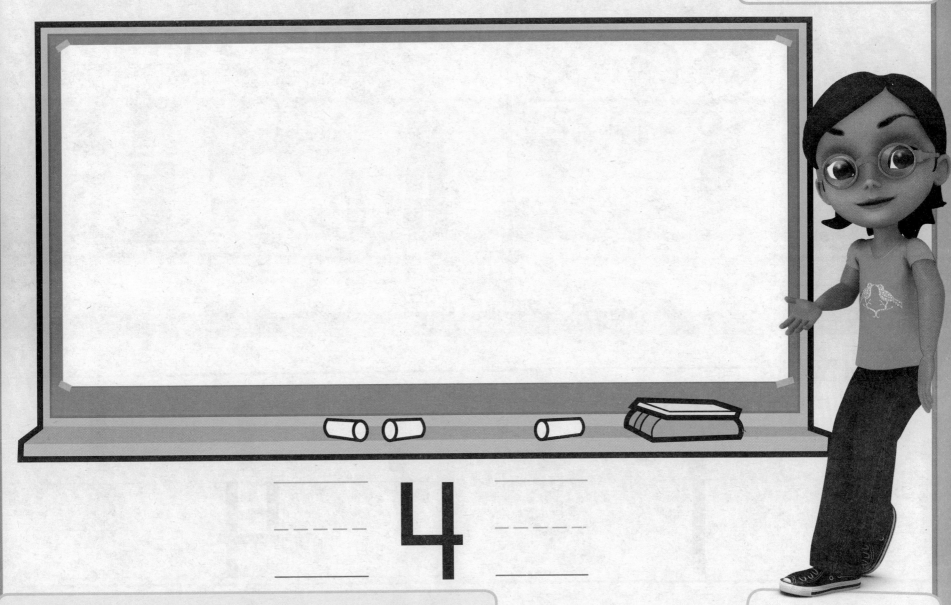

4

Directions Say: *Marta is thinking of two numbers—one is the number that comes just before 4 when counting, and the other is the number that comes just after 4 when counting. Write the two numbers Marta is thinking of. Show how you know you are correct.*

I can ...
count up to the number 5.

I can also use math tools correctly.

☆ Guided Practice

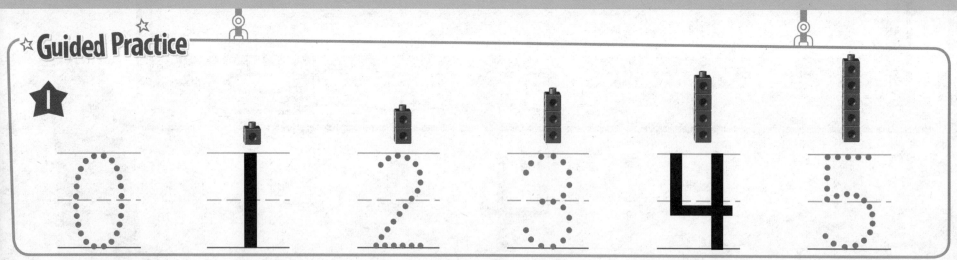

1

0   1   2   4   5

Directions ⭐ Have students write the number that comes just before 1 when counting, and the number that comes just after 1 when counting. Then have them write the number that comes just before 4 when counting, and the number that comes just after 4 when counting. Have them count the numbers in order from 0 to 5.

Name _____

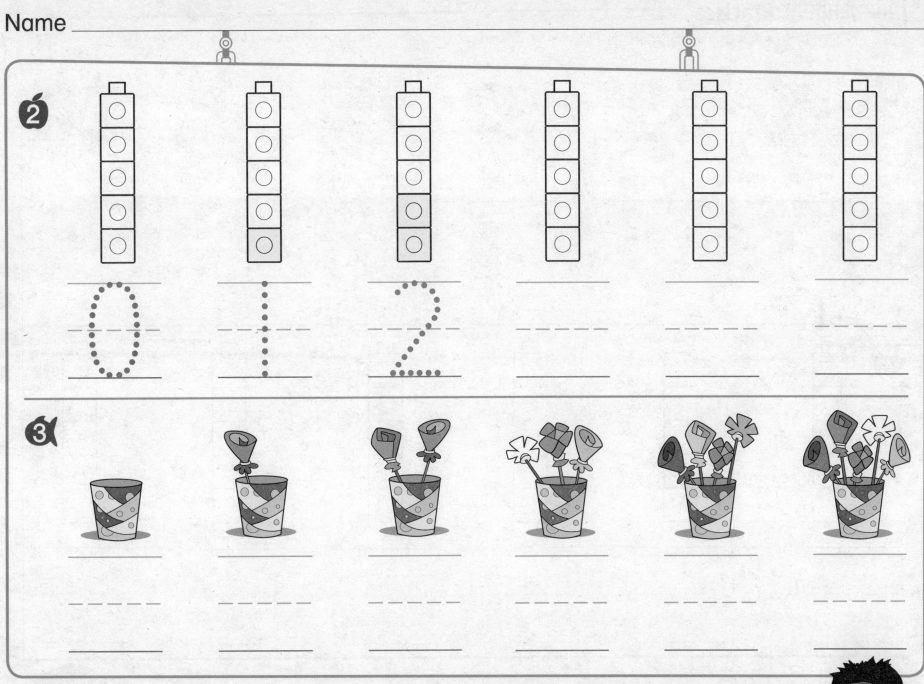

2

0   1   2

3

Directions Have students: **2** color the cubes to show each number, write the numbers in order, and then draw a circle around the number that comes just after 1 when counting; **3** count the flowers in each vase, write the numbers, and then count the numbers in order from 0 to 5.

Independent Practice

💜 4

_____

- - - - - - - - - - - -

_____

✋5

_____

- - - - - - - - - - - -

_____

Directions ♥ Have students count the toys in each box, write the numbers, and then draw a circle around the number that comes just after 4 when counting. ✋ **Higher Order Thinking** Have students color 5 cubes, and then write the number. Have them color to show the number that comes just before it when counting in the next tower, and then write the number. Repeat for the remaining towers.

Name _____

Another Look!

HOME ACTIVITY Ask your child to count the numbers from 0 to 5 in order, and then count backward from 5 to 0.

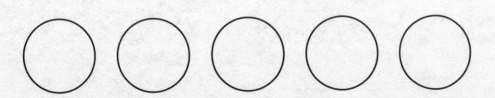

Directions Say: *The first row has zero counters colored. Write the number to tell how many. The next row shows 1 more counter colored. Write the number to tell how many.* ⭐ *and* ❷ *Have students color counters to add 1 more counter to each row than the row before, and then write the number to tell how many.*

③

◯ ◯ ◯ ◯ ◯

‒ ‒ ‒ ‒

——————

④

◯ ◯ ◯ ◯ ◯

‒ ‒ ‒ ‒

——————

✋5

‒ ‒ ‒ ‒   ‒ ‒ ‒ ‒   ‒ ‒ ‒ ‒   ‒ ‒ ‒ ‒   ‒ ‒ ‒ ‒   ‒ ‒ ‒ ‒

——————   ——————   ——————   ——————   ——————   ——————

6

‒ ‒ ‒ ‒   ‒ ‒ ‒ ‒   ‒ ‒ ‒ ‒   ‒ ‒ ‒ ‒   ‒ ‒ ‒ ‒   ‒ ‒ ‒ ‒

——————   ——————   ——————   ——————   ——————   ——————

Directions ③ and ④ Have students color counters to add I more counter to each row than the counters in the item before, and then write the number to tell how many. ✋ **Number Sense** Have students write the numbers in order from 0 to 5, draw a circle around the number that comes just before I when counting, and then mark an X on the number that comes just after I when counting. 6 **Higher Order Thinking** Have students count backward from 5 to 0, and then write the numbers.

Topic I | Lesson 10

Solve & Share

Name _____

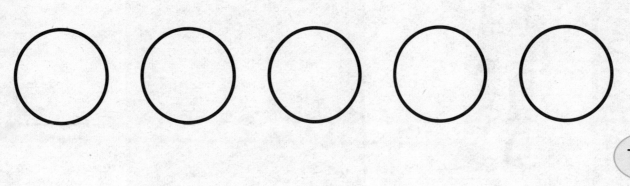

Think.

_____

- - - - -

_____

Directions Say: *Alex needs to count the group of shapes. How can you count these shapes? Use objects or words to help. Write the number to tell how many shapes. Tell why your number is correct.*

I can ...
use math to explain what I know about counting.

I can also count to 5.

Topic 1 | Lesson 11

Digital Resources at SavvasRealize.com

sixty-seven **67**

How can I explain?

1 2 3

Numbers

3

☆ Guided Practice

1

2

Directions ⭐ and ❷ Have students make a math argument about how many birds are in each row, and then write the number. Have them use objects, words, or a method of their choice to explain their arguments and tell why they are correct.

Topic I | Lesson 11

Tools Assessment

Independent Practice

3

4

5

6

Directions 3–5 Have students make a math argument about how many leaves are in each row, and then write the number. Have them use objects, words, or a method of their choice to explain their arguments and tell why they are correct.
6 Math and Science Say: *Chlorophyll makes leaves green. There is less sunlight in the winter, so trees save their chlorophyll. This turns leaves brown, orange, red, and yellow.* Have students make a math argument about how many orange leaves are in the row, and then write the number. Have them use objects, words, or a method of their choice to explain their arguments and tell why they are correct.

Topic 1 | Lesson 11

sixty-nine **69**

Problem Solving

_____

- - - - - - - -

_____

Name _____

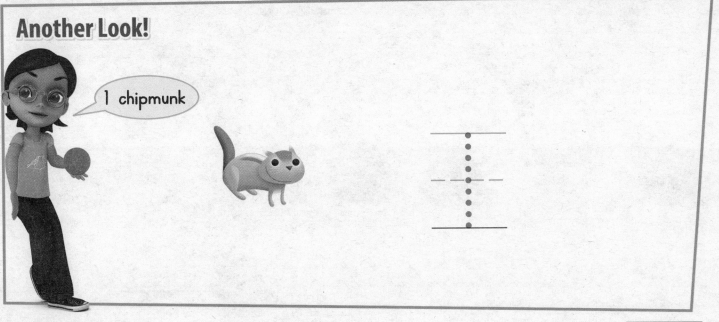

Another Look!

1 chipmunk

HOME ACTIVITY Place a row of up to 5 cups in front of your child. Have your child count the number of cups, write the number, and explain why his or her number is correct. Repeat with different numbers of cups up to 5.

1

_____

2

_____

3

_____

Directions Say: *Marta places 1 counter on the chipmunk and argues that there is 1 chipmunk. Practice writing the number to tell how many.* **1**–**3** Have students make a math argument about how many chipmunks are in each row, and then write the number. Have them use objects, words, or a method of their choice to explain their arguments and tell why they are correct.

Name _____

⭐ 1

A   **2**

🍎 2

_____
- - - - - - - -
_____

🌼 3

2   **4**

♥ 4

Directions **Understand Vocabulary** Have students: ⭐ draw a circle around the **number**; 🍎 write the number that means **none**; 🌼 draw a circle around the number **four**; ♥ mark an X on a **part**, and then draw a circle around the **whole**.

5   1   **3**

6

_____

- - - - - - - - -

_____

7

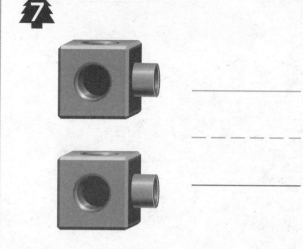

_____

- - - - - - - - -

_____

8

_____ _____ _____ _____ _____

- - - - - - - - - - - - - - - - - - - - - - - - -

_____ _____ _____ _____ _____

Directions   **Understand Vocabulary**   Have students: **5** draw a circle around the number **one**; **6** write the number **three**; **7** **count** the number of cubes, and then write the number to tell how many; **8** write the numbers 0 to 5 in **order**, and then draw counters to show that many of each number.

Topic I | Vocabulary Review

Name ______________________________

TOPIC 1

Reteaching

Set A

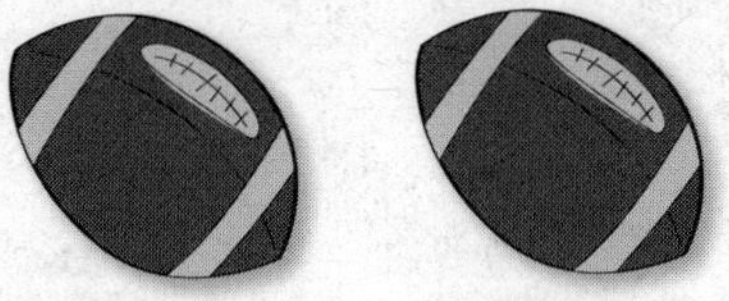

1 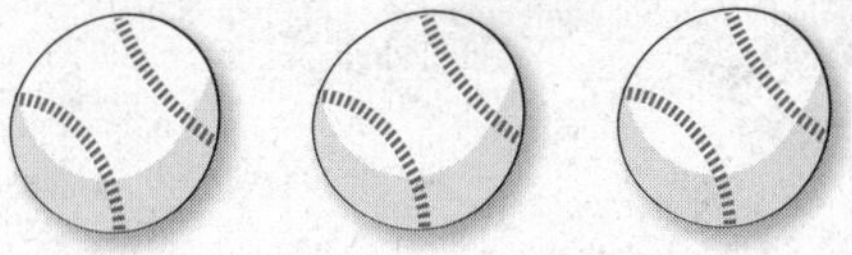

2 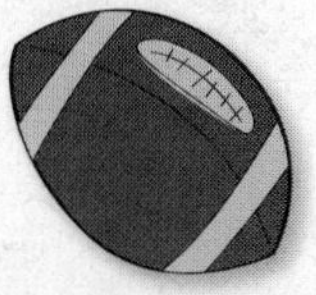

Set B

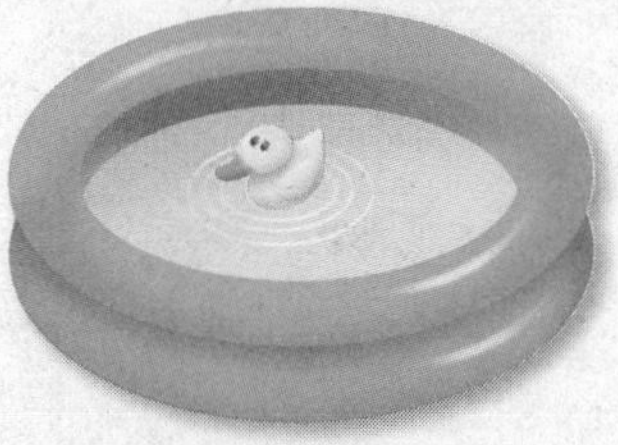

1

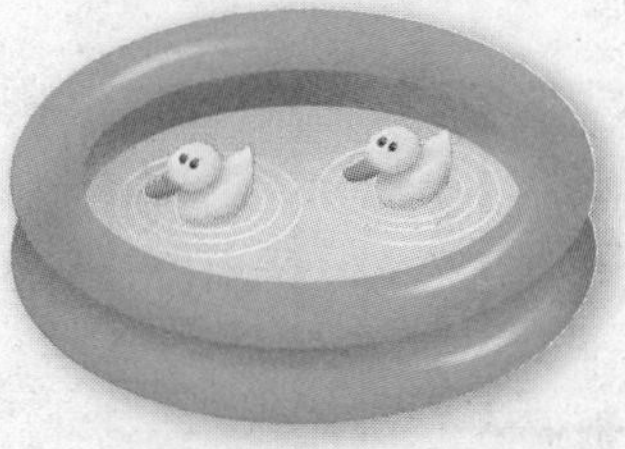

2

3 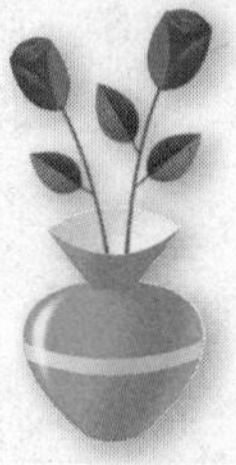

4 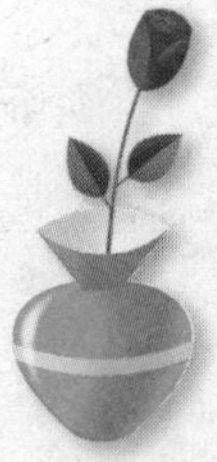

Directions Have students: 1 and 2 color a box as they count each ball to show how many; 3 and 4 count the flowers in the vase, and then practice writing the number that tells how many.

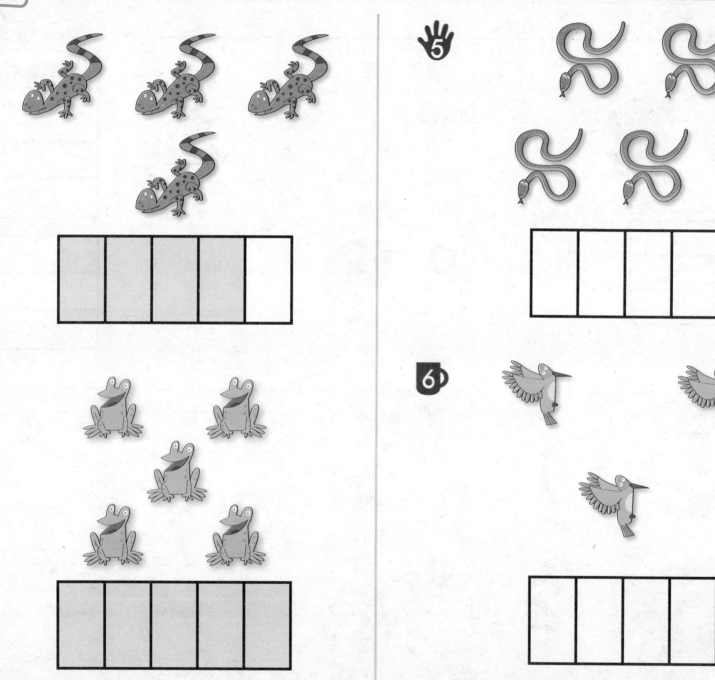

Directions 🖐 and 👆 Have students color a box as they count each animal to show how many.

Topic 1 | Reteaching

Name _____

_____

3 and **2**

🌲7

_____ and _____

_____

0

🏴8

◆9

_____

_____

Directions Have students: 🌲 use gray and brown crayons to color the animals to show a different way to make 5, and then write the numbers to tell how many gray and how many brown dogs; 🏴 and ◆ count the flowers in the vase, and then practice writing the number that tells how many.

4

_____

- - - - - - - - - -

_____

3

_____

- - - - - - - - - -

_____

Directions 🏠 and ✿ Have students count the octopuses, and then practice writing the number that tells how many.

78 seventy-eight

Name _____

⭐ 1

Ⓐ

Ⓑ

Ⓒ

Ⓓ

🍎 2

☐

☐

☐

☐

⭐ 3

2   3   4   5
Ⓐ   Ⓑ   Ⓒ   Ⓓ

♥ 4

Ⓐ   Ⓑ   Ⓒ   Ⓓ

Directions Have students mark the best answer. ⭐ Which shows 3 flowers? 🍎 Mark all the ways that do NOT show a way to make 5. ⭐ How many pears are there? ♥ Which box has 0 toys in it?

✋ **5**

🍵 **6**

🌲 **7**

Directions Have students: ✋ make a math argument about how many leaves are in each row, and then write the number; 🍵 count the butterflies, and then color the boxes to show how many; 🌲 count the number of dots and then draw counters in the box to show the same number of dots.

Topic I | Assessment

Name _____

8 ❋   ❋❋   ❋❋❋   ❋❋❋❋   ❋❋❋❋❋

___   ___   ___   ___   ___

_ _ _ _   _ _ _ _   _ _ _ _   _ _ _ _   _ _ _ _

___   ___   ___   ___   ___

9

_____   _____

_ _ _ _ _   _ _ _ _ _

_____ and _____

Directions Have students: **8** count the snowflakes, and then write the number to tell how many; **9** color the leaves red and yellow to show a way to make 5, and then write the numbers to tell how many yellow and how many red leaves.

_____

_ _ _ _ _

_____

_____

_ _ _ _ _

_____

Directions Have students: count the plates, and then write the number to tell how many; ✿ count the number of apples on the plate, and then color the apples to show how many; ✌ draw 5 marbles, and then write the number to tell how many.

Copyright © Savvas Learning Company LLC. All Rights Reserved.

Topic 1 | Assessment

Name _____

★ I

_____

- - - - - - - - -

_____

- - - - - - - - -

_____

- - - - - - - - -

_____

- - - - - - - - -

_____

Directions **Flower Cart** Say: *Michael's family sells flowers from a flower cart.* ★ Have students count how many of each kind of flower, and then write the number to tell how many.

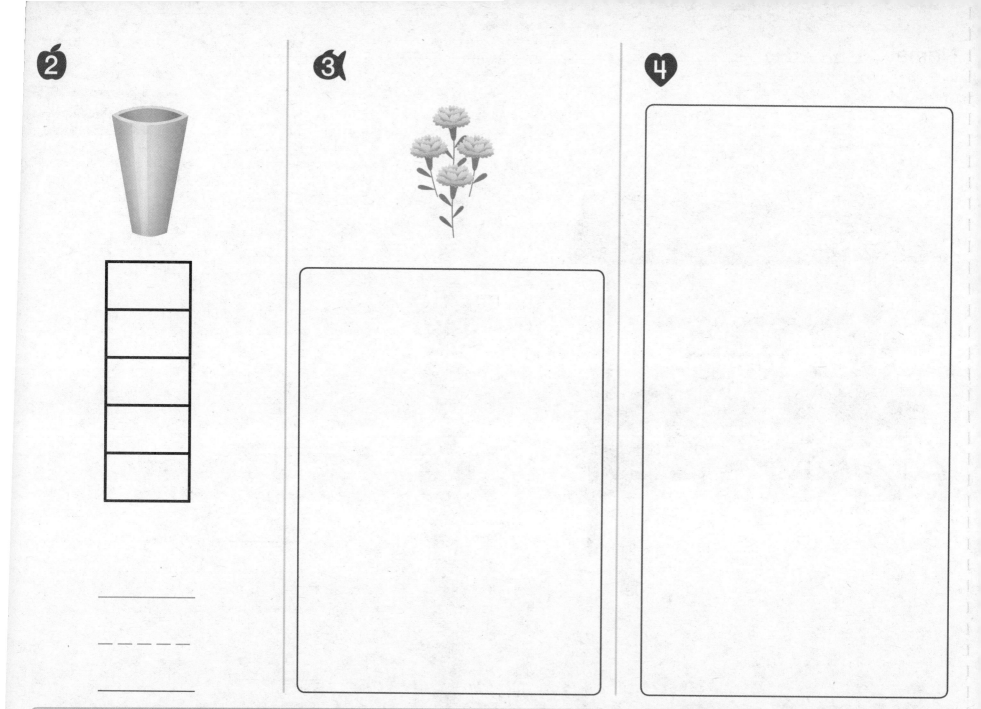

2

3

4

Topic 1 | Performance Assessment

Compare Numbers 0 to 5

Essential Question: How can numbers from 0 to 5 be compared and ordered?

Digital Resources

Solve · Learn · Glossary

Tools · Assessment · Help · Games

Snow

Be careful.

Math and Science Project: Severe Weather

Directions Read the character speech bubbles to students. **Find Out!** Have students name different types of severe weather that occur around the world. Say: *Not all places have the same types of severe weather. Talk to your friends and relatives about severe weather that has happened in the world in the past month. Ask them if they have ever seen that type of severe weather.* **Journal: Make a Poster** Have students make a poster. Ask them to draw up to 5 items people might need to be safe in a snowstorm. Have them draw up to 5 items people might need to be safe during a drought. Ask them to write the number of objects in each group, compare them, and then draw a circle around the number that is greater than the other number.

Name _____

Review What You Know

  1

0	2

2

3	1

3

4	5

4

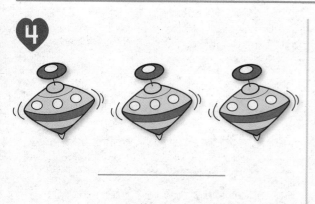

_ _ _ _ _ _ _ _

_____

5

_ _ _ _ _ _ _ _

_____

6

_ _ _ _ _ _ _ _

_____

Directions Have students cut out the vocabulary cards. Read the front of the card, and then ask them to explain what the word or phrase means.

A-Z
Glossary

equal

same number as

compare

group

greater than

less than

My Word Cards

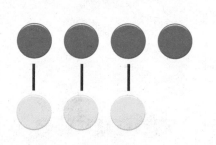

Point to the picture.
Say: *When we **compare** these groups, we see that they each have a different amount of counters.*

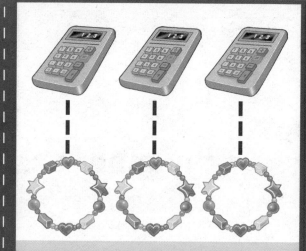

Point to the picture.
Say: *The top group has the **same number as** the bottom group.*

Point to the picture.
Say: *Both groups have 3 counters. They are **equal**.*

Point to the 3.
Say: *3 is **less than** 4.*

Point to the 4.
Say: *4 is **greater than** 3.*

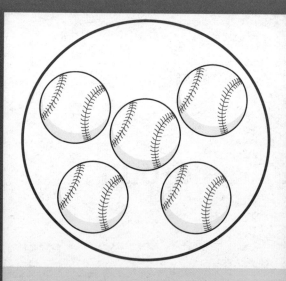

Point to the baseballs.
Say: *This is a **group** of baseballs.*

My Word Cards

Directions Have students cut out the vocabulary cards. Read the front of the card, and then ask them to explain what the word or phrase means.

model

My Word Cards

Point to the part-part model.
Say: **Models** help us represent number or word problems.

Directions Say: *Marta has some toy cars. Are there the same number of red cars as there are yellow cars on the rug? How do you know? Use counters to show your work.*

I can ...
compare groups to see whether they are equal by matching.

I can also reason about math.

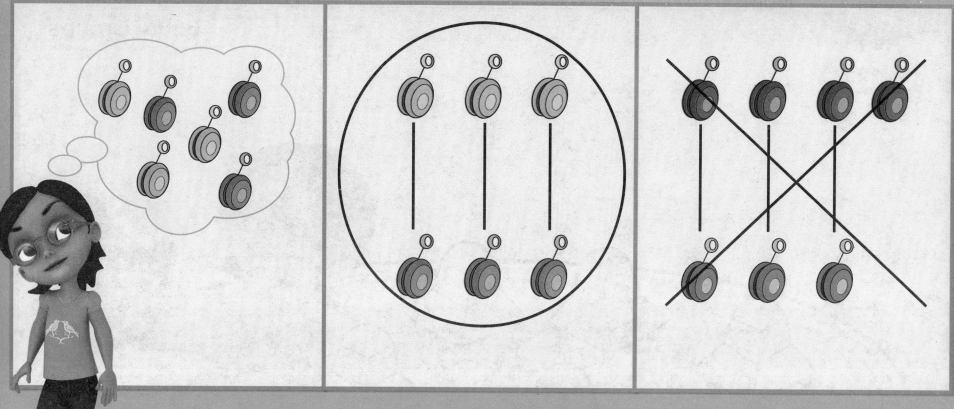

☆ Guided Practice

1

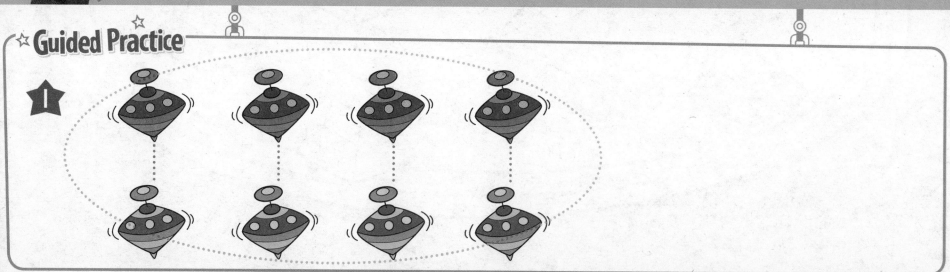

Directions ⭐ Have students draw lines between the toys in the top group to the toys in the bottom group. Then have them draw a circle around the groups if they are equal in number, or mark an X on the groups if they are NOT equal in number.

92 ninety-two

Topic 2 | Lesson 1

Name _____

2

3

4

5

Directions 🍎–✋ Have students draw lines from the blocks in one group to the blocks in the other group. Then have them draw a circle around the groups if they are equal in number, or mark an X on the groups if they are NOT equal in number.

Topic 2 | Lesson 1   ninety-three **93**

Independent Practice

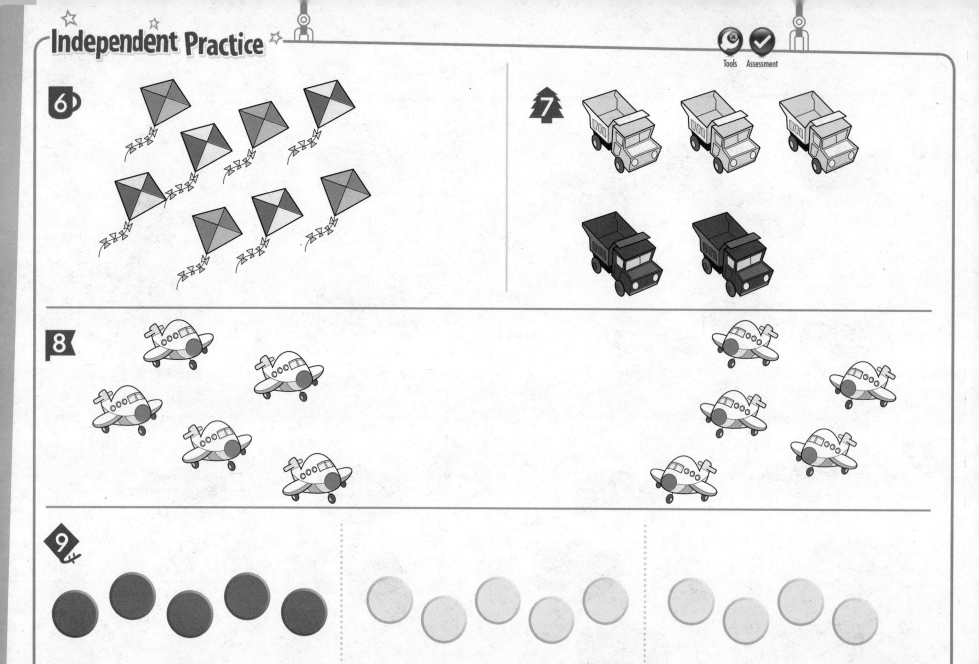

6

7

8

9

Directions 6–8 Have students draw lines from the toys in one group to the toys in the other group. Then have them draw a circle around the groups if they are equal in number, or mark an X on the groups if they are NOT equal in number.
9 **Higher Order Thinking** Have students draw a circle around the group of yellow counters that is NOT equal in number to the group of red counters.

Topic 2 | Lesson 1

Name _____

Another Look!

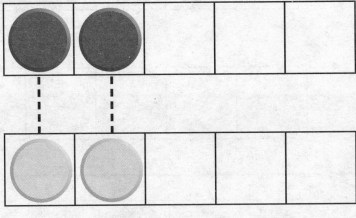

HOME ACTIVITY Give your child 5 objects. Place up to 5 objects on the table. Ask your child to make a group of objects that is equal in number to the group you made. Repeat with different numbers of objects. (Object suggestions: forks/spoons; pencils/pens)

⭐ 1

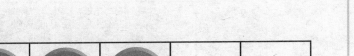

🍎 2

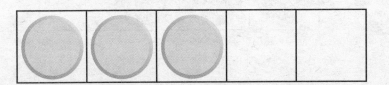

Directions Say: *How can you show that the group of yellow counters is equal in number to the group of red counters? Draw lines to match the counters from one group to the other group.* ⭐ and 🍎 Have students draw lines to match the counters from one group to the other group. Then have them draw a circle around the groups if they are equal in number, or mark an X on the groups if they are NOT equal in number.

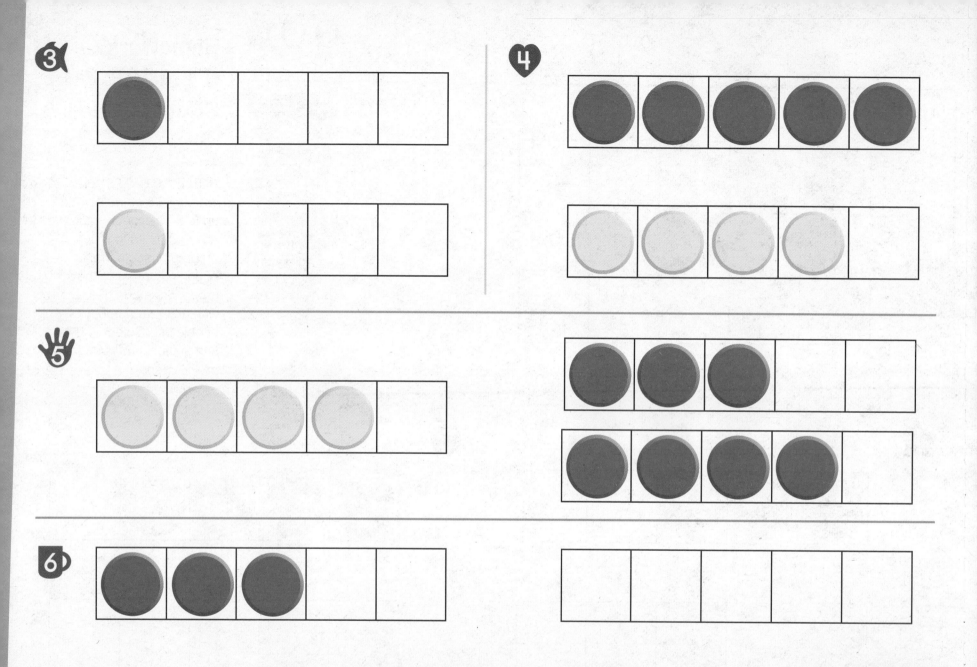

3

4

5

6

Topic 2 | Lesson 1

Name _____

Solve

Directions Say: *Marta's class goes to the park. Mr. Leeman brings 4 soccer balls and 3 basketballs. Which group of balls has more? How do you know? Use counters to show your work.*

I can …
tell whether one group is greater in number than another group.

I can also reason about math.

Digital Resources at SavvasRealize.com

ninety-seven **97**

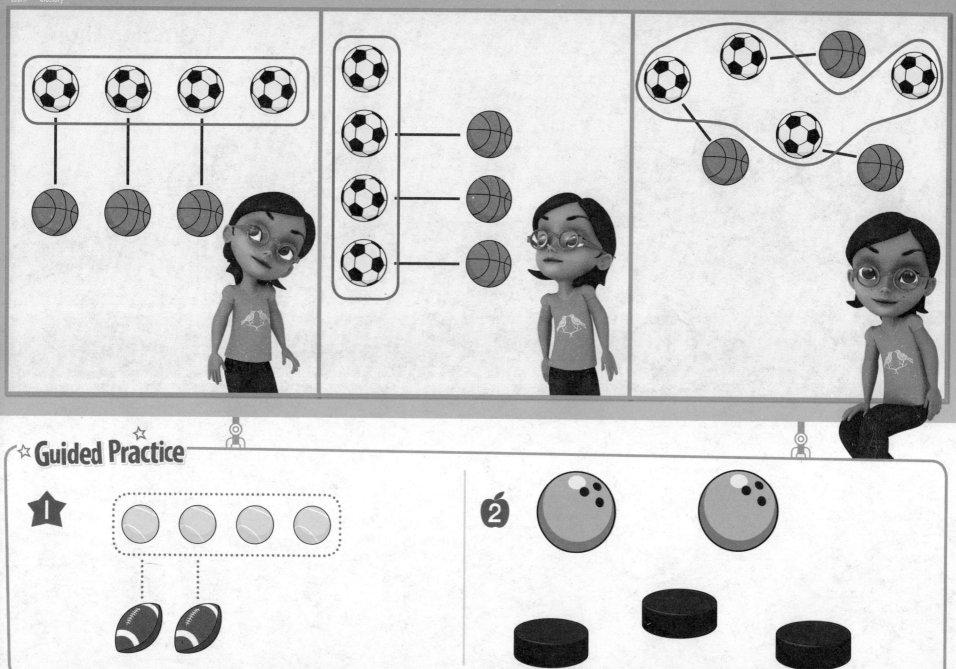

☆ Guided Practice

1

2

Directions 🡑 and ✌ Have students draw lines to match objects from one group to the other group. Have them draw a circle around the group that is greater in number than the other group, and then explain why they are correct.

98 ninety-eight

Copyright © Savvas Learning Company LLC. All Rights Reserved.

Topic 2 | Lesson 2

Name _____

3

4

5

Directions **3–5** Have students draw lines to match objects from one group to the other group. Have them draw a circle around the group that is greater in number than the other group, and then explain why they are correct.

Topic 2 | Lesson 2

ninety-nine **99**

Independent Practice

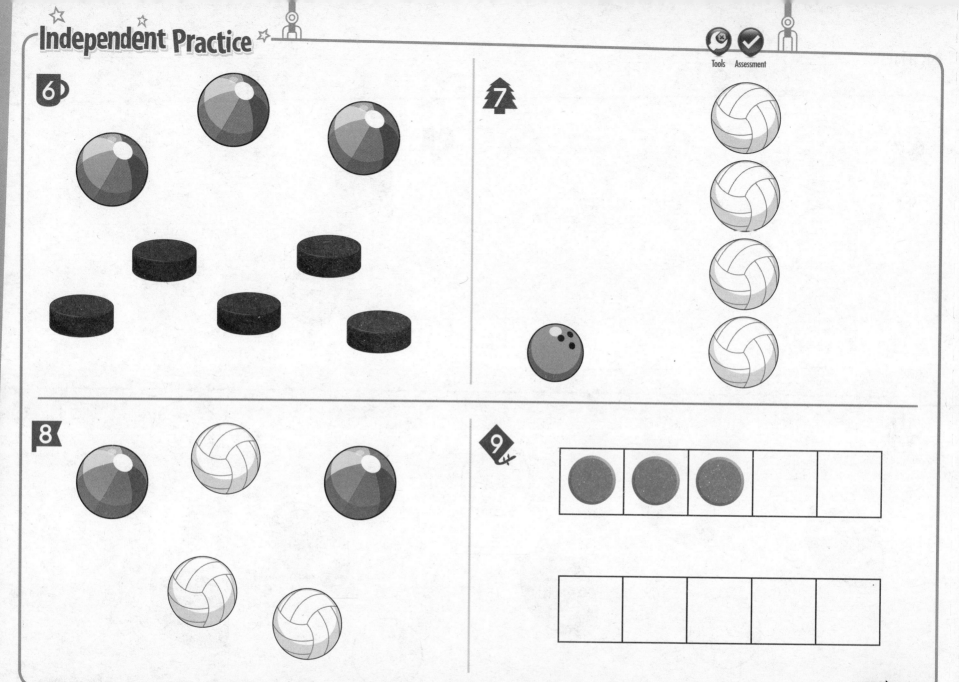

6

7

8

9

Directions 6–8 Have students draw lines to match objects from one group to the other group. Have them draw a circle around the group that is greater in number than the other group, and then explain why they are correct. **9 Higher Order Thinking** Have students draw a group of counters in the bottom five-frame that is greater in number than the group of counters in the top five-frame. Have them explain their drawings.

100 one hundred

Topic 2 | Lesson 2

Name _____

 **Another Look!**

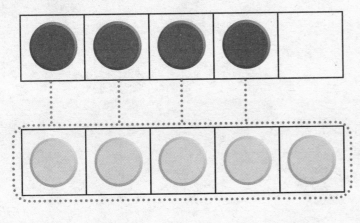

HOME ACTIVITY Give your child 5 objects. Place up to 4 objects on the table. Ask your child to make a group that is greater in number than the group you made. Repeat with different numbers of objects.

 1

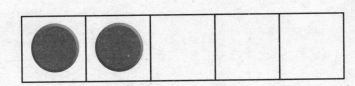

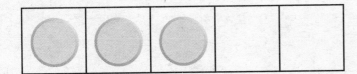

2

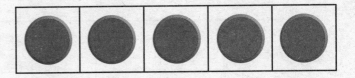

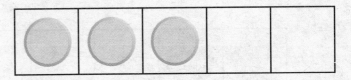

Directions Say: *How do you know which group of counters, the red or the yellow, is greater in number than the other? Draw a line from each red counter to a yellow counter. Draw a circle around the group that has counters left over.* ⭐ and ❷ Have students draw lines to match the red and yellow groups of counters. Have them draw a circle around the group that is greater in number than the other group, and then explain why they are correct.

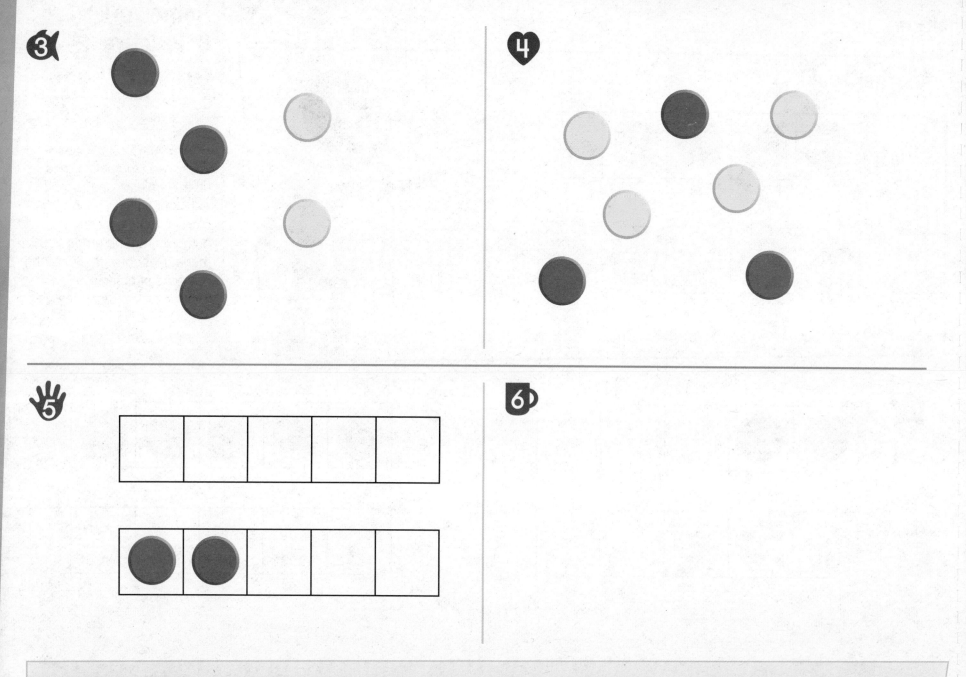

Directions ❸ and ❹ Have students draw lines to match the red and yellow groups of counters. Have them draw a circle around the group that is greater in number than the other group, and then explain why they are correct. ✋ **Vocabulary** Have students draw a number of counters in the top five-frame that is greater than the number of counters in the bottom five-frame, and then explain how they know. ❻ **Higher Order Thinking** Have students draw two different groups of counters or objects. Have them show and explain which group is greater in number than the other group.

 **Solve & Share**

Name _____

Solve

Lesson 2-3
Less Than

Directions Say: *Marta puts 5 stuffed animals on a shelf. She puts 3 teddy bears on a different shelf. Which group has fewer stuffed toys? How do you know? Use counters to show your work.*

I can ... tell whether one group is less in number than another group.

I can also reason about math.

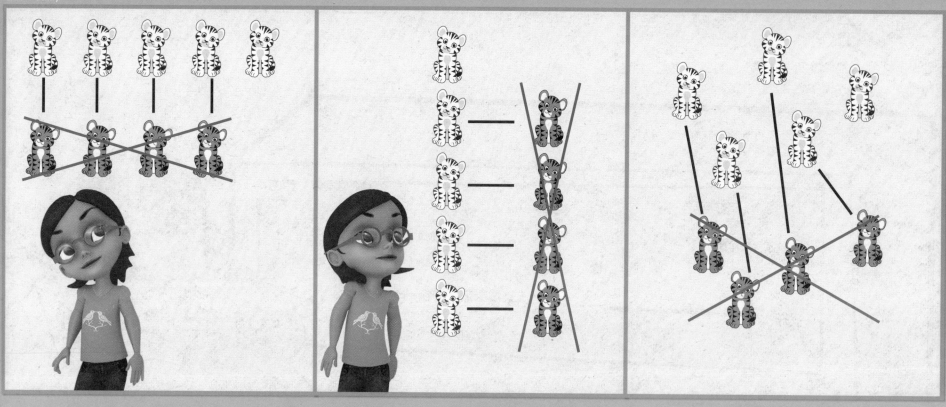

☆ Guided Practice

1

2

Directions 1 and 2 Have students draw lines to match the toys from one group to the other group. Have them mark an X on the group that is less in number than the other group, and then explain why they are correct.

Topic 2 | Lesson 3

Name _____

Directions 🔵–✋ Have students draw lines to match the toys from one group to the other group. Have them mark an X on the group that is less in number than the other group, and then explain why they are correct.

Topic 2 | Lesson 3

one hundred five **105**

Independent Practice

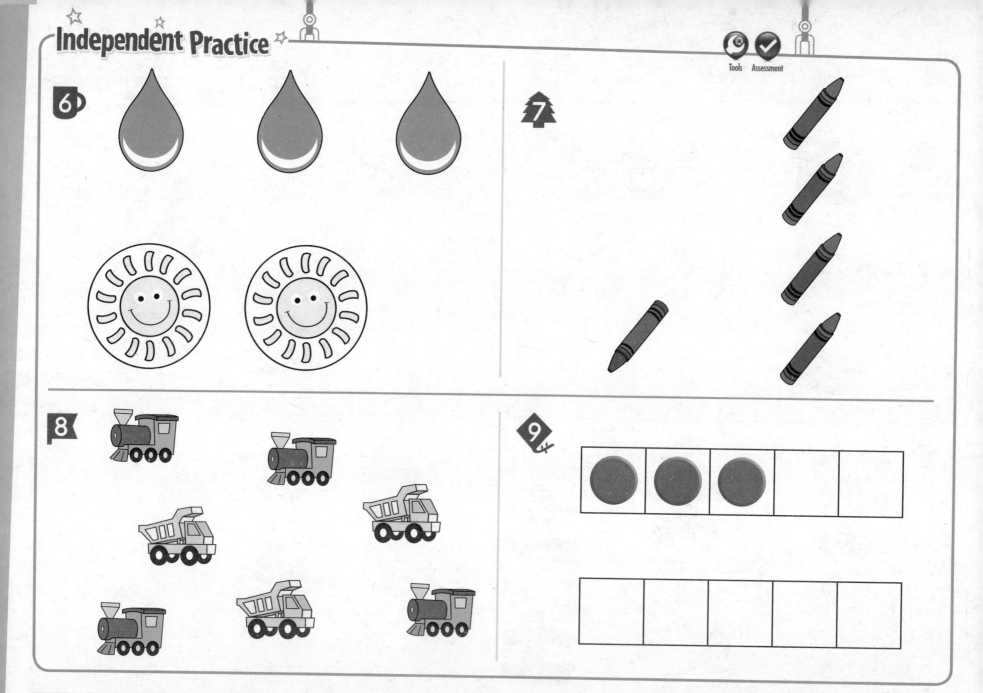

Directions ✎ **Math and Science** Ask students what a raindrop means in a weather forecast. Have students draw lines between groups to match the raindrop stickers to the sun stickers. Have them mark an X on the group that is less in number than the other group, and then explain why they are correct. ✎ and ✎ Have students draw lines to match the objects from one group to the other group. Have them mark an X on the group that is less in number than the other group, and then explain why they are correct. ✎ **Higher Order Thinking** Have students draw a group of yellow counters that is less in number than the group of red counters.

Topic 2 | Lesson 3

Name _____

Another Look!

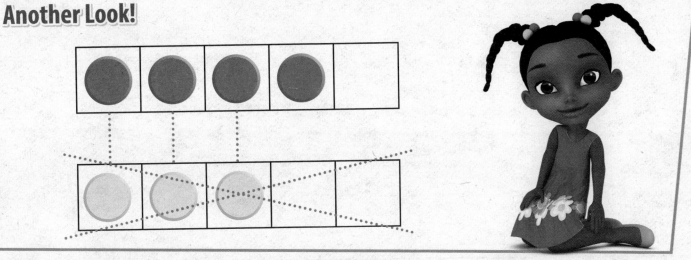

HOME ACTIVITY Give your child 5 objects. Place at least 2 objects on the table. Ask your child to make a group that is less in number than the group you made. Repeat with different numbers of objects.

 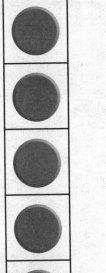 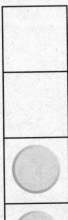

2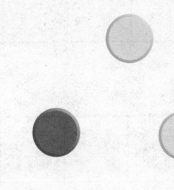

Directions Say: *How do you know which group of counters, the red or the yellow, is less in number than the other? Draw a line from each red counter to a yellow counter. Mark an X on the group that is less in number.* ⭐ *and* **2** *Have students draw lines to match counters from one group to the other group. Have them mark an X on the group that is less in number than the other group, and then explain why they are correct.*

Topic 2 | Lesson 3   Digital Resources at SavvasRealize.com   one hundred seven   **107**

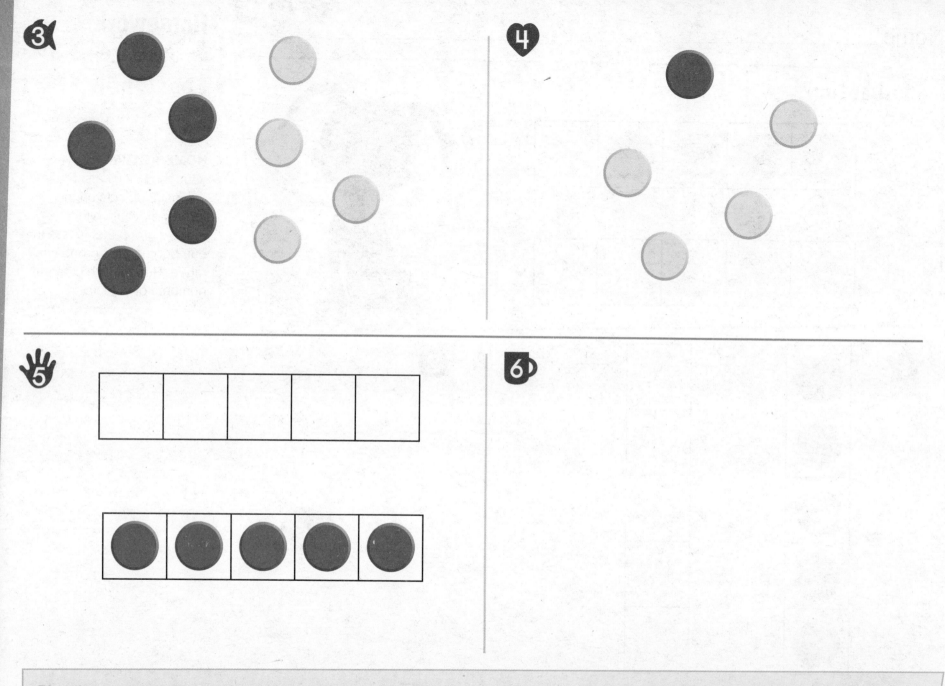

3

4

5

6

Solve & Share

Name _____

Solve

Directions Say: *Marta puts a group of elephant stickers on one page of her sticker book. She puts a group of lion stickers on another page. Compare the groups. Write the numbers to tell how many. Then draw a circle around the number of the group of stickers that is greater than the other group.*

I can ... compare groups by counting.

I can also be precise in my work.

Topic 2 | Lesson 4

Digital Resources at SavvasRealize.com

one hundred nine 109

☆ Guided Practice

1

Directions ★ Have students count the monkey and banana stickers, and then write the numbers to tell how many. Then have them draw a circle around the number that is greater than the other number and mark an X on the number that is less than the other number.

Topic 2 | Lesson 4

Name _____

2

3

4

5

Directions **2**–**5** Have students count the stickers, write the numbers to tell how many, and then draw a circle around the number that is greater than the other number and mark an X on the number that is less than the other number, or draw a circle around both numbers if they are equal.

Independent Practice

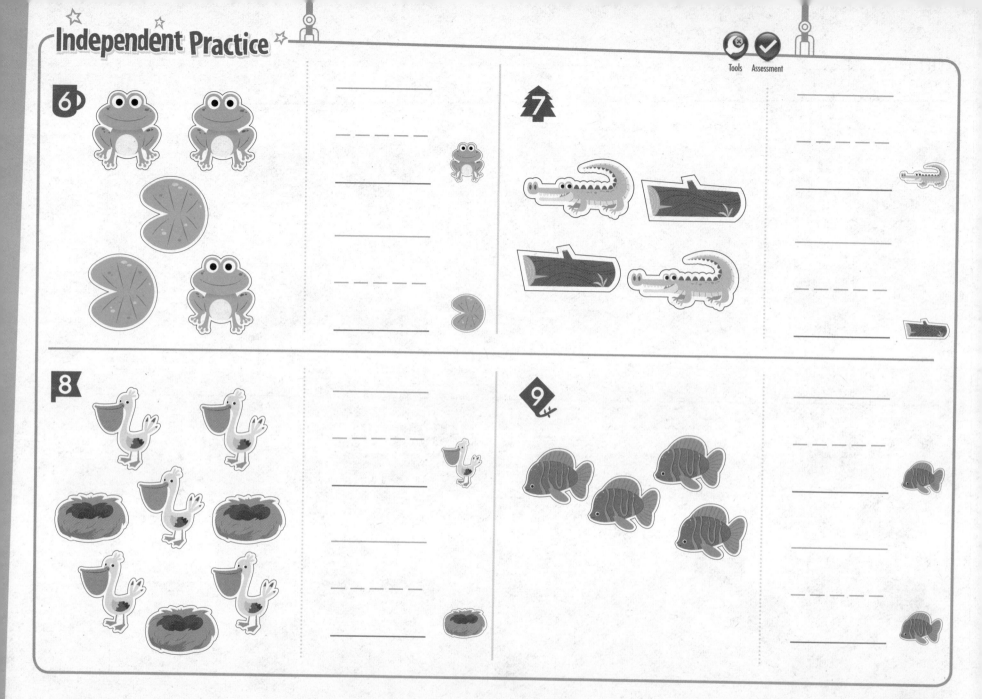

6

7

8

9

Directions **6–8** Have students count the stickers, write the numbers to tell how many, and then draw a circle around the number that is greater than the other number and mark an X on the number that is less than the other number, or draw a circle around both numbers if they are equal. **Higher Order Thinking** Have students count the fish stickers, draw a group of fish stickers that is less in number than the group shown, and then write the numbers to tell how many.

Topic 2 | **Lesson 4**

Name _____

Another Look!

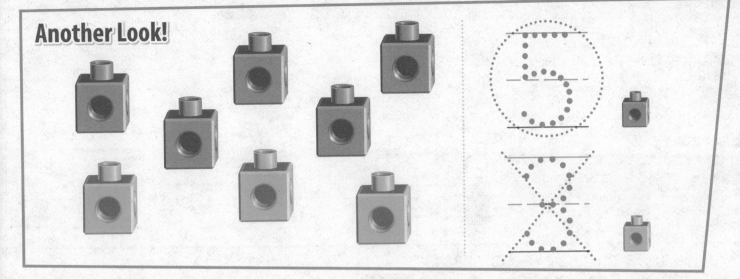

HOME ACTIVITY Gather 10 objects, such as buttons or straws. Show 4 objects randomly on a table. Ask your child to make a group of 2 objects. Have him or her write numbers to tell how many are in each group, and then explain which group is greater in number and which group is less in number.

⭐ 1   ② 2

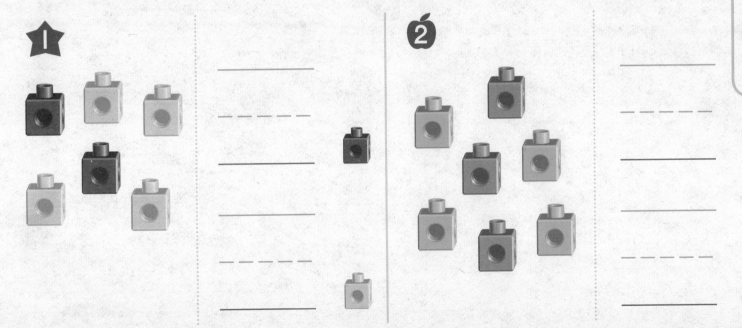

Directions Say: *You can count the blue and green cubes to find out which group is greater in number. Count the cubes, and then write the numbers to tell how many. Draw a circle around the number that is greater than the other number and mark an X on the number that is less than the other number.* ⭐ and ② *Have students count the cubes, write the numbers to tell how many, and then draw a circle around the number that is greater than the other number and mark an X on the number that is less than the other number.*

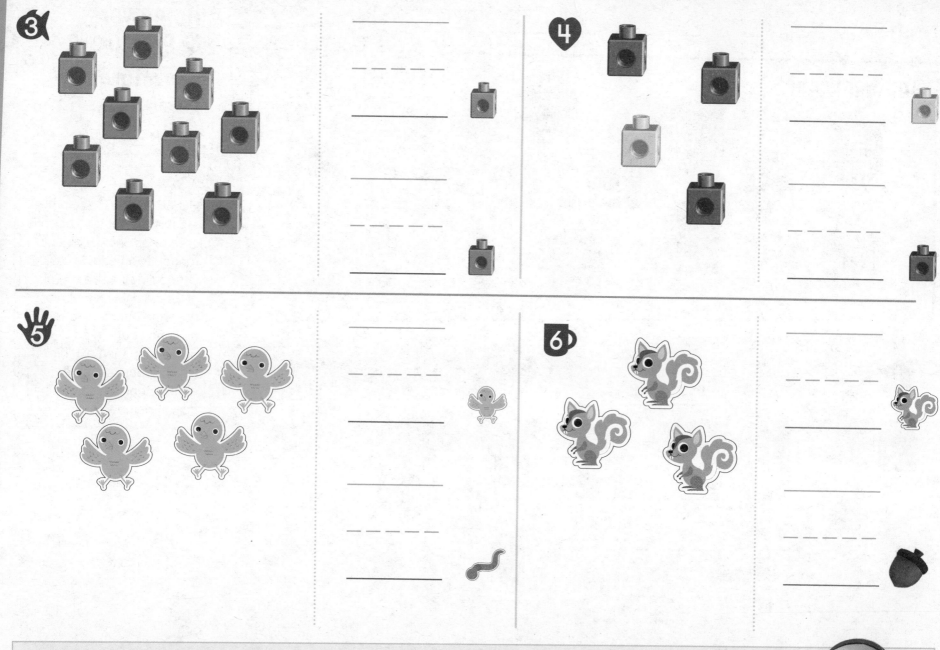

3

4

5

6

Directions **3** and **4** Have students count the cubes, write the numbers to tell how many, and then draw a circle around the number that is greater than the other number and mark an X on the number that is less than the other number. **5** **Higher Order Thinking** Have students count the bird stickers, draw a group of worms that is less in number than the group of birds shown, and then write the numbers to tell how many. **6** **Higher Order Thinking** Have students count the squirrel stickers, draw a group of nuts equal in number to the group of squirrels shown, and then write the numbers to tell how many.

Solve & Share

Name _____

Solve

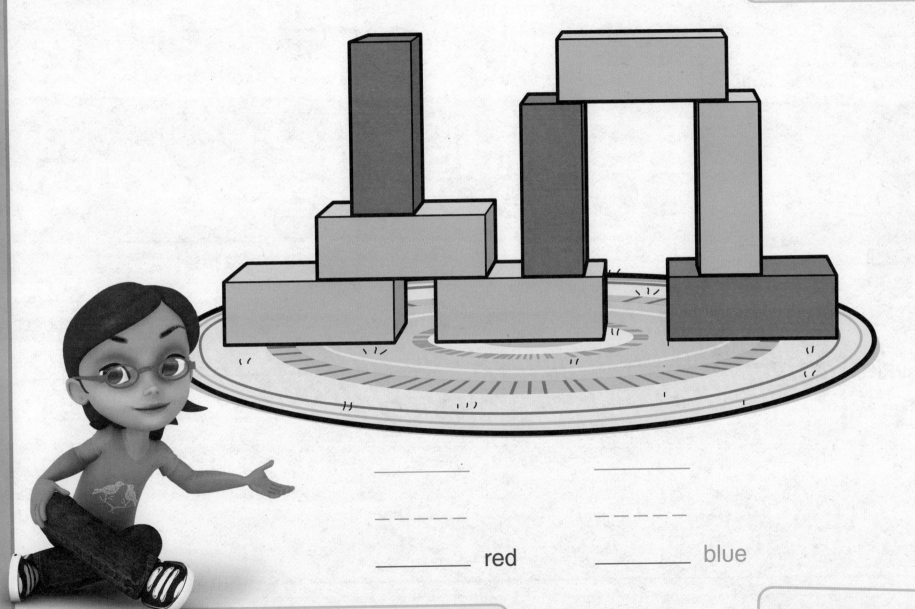

_____ .   _____ .

- - - - - - -   - - - - - - -

_____ red   _____ blue

Directions Say: Marta builds a tower with red and blue blocks. Count how many red blocks and how many blue blocks she uses. Write the numbers to tell how many. Then draw a circle around the number that is less than the other number.

I can ...
compare numbers.

I can also reason about math.

Topic 2 | Lesson 5
Digital Resources at SavvasRealize.com
one hundred fifteen   **115**

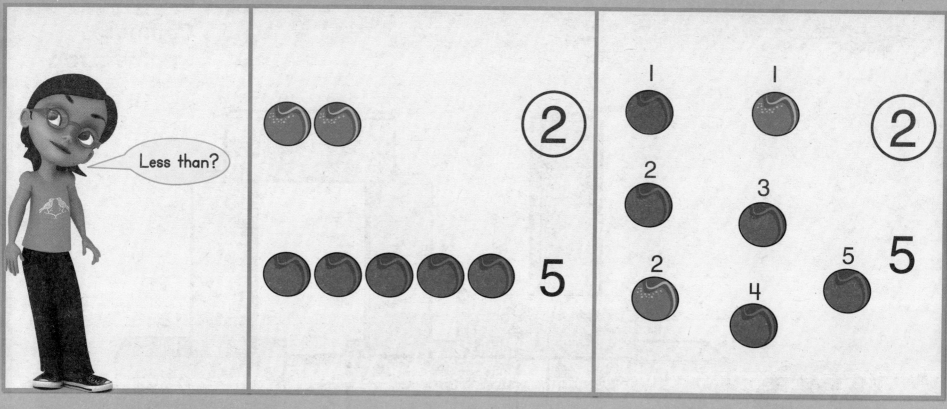

Less than?

2

5

1   1

2   3

2   4   5   5

☆ Guided Practice

⭐1   1

4

2   3

2

116   one hundred sixteen

Name _____

❸ 5

3

♥ 2

2

✋ 0

1

☕ 4

3

Directions Have students compare the numbers. Then have them: **❸** and **♥** draw a circle around the number that is greater than the other number, or draw a circle around both numbers if they are equal. Have students draw pictures to show how they know; **✋** and **☕** mark an X on the number that is less than the other number, or draw a circle around both numbers if they are equal. Have students draw pictures to show how they know.

Topic 2 | Lesson 5

one hundred seventeen **117**

Tools Assessment

7 3

1

8 4

2

9 [5]

10 [2]

Directions Have students compare the numbers. Then have them: **7** mark an X on the number that is less than the other number, or draw a circle around both numbers if they are equal. Have students draw pictures to show how they know; **8** draw a circle around the number that is greater than the other number, or draw a circle around both numbers if they are equal. Have students draw pictures to show how they know. **9 Higher Order Thinking** Have students look at the number card, and then write the number that is equal to that number. Then have them draw pictures to show how many. **10 Higher Order Thinking** Have students look at the number card, and then write a number that is less than that number. Then have them draw pictures to show how many.

Topic 2 | Lesson 5

Name _____

Another Look!

2

5

HOME ACTIVITY Write two numbers between 0 and 5. Ask your child to compare the numbers. Have him or her point to the number that is greater than the other number. If needed, have your child use household objects, such as buttons or straws, to help show how many.

3

2

 2

4

4

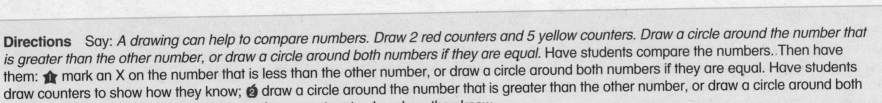
Directions Say: *A drawing can help to compare numbers. Draw 2 red counters and 5 yellow counters. Draw a circle around the number that is greater than the other number, or draw a circle around both numbers if they are equal.* Have students compare the numbers. Then have them: mark an X on the number that is less than the other number, or draw a circle around both numbers if they are equal. Have students draw counters to show how they know; draw a circle around the number that is greater than the other number, or draw a circle around both numbers if they are equal. Have students draw counters to show how they know.

3 2

0

4 5

3

5 4

6 3

Name _____

Think.

Directions Say: *Work with your partner and take turns. Take I cube at a time from the bag and place it on your mat. Keep taking cubes until all the cubes are gone. Do you have a greater number of red cubes or blue cubes? How can you show your answer? Explain and show your work.*

I can ...
use objects, drawings, and numbers to compare numbers.

I can also write numbers to 5.

Topic 2 | Lesson 6

Digital Resources at SavvasRealize.com

one hundred twenty-one **121**

☆ Guided Practice

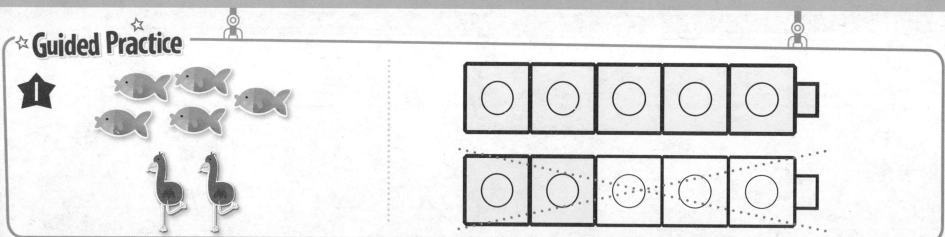

Directions ⭐ Say: *Marta has 5 fish stickers and 2 flamingo stickers. Which group of stickers is less in number than the other group? How can you use cubes to show how to find the answer?* Have students create cube trains for each group, color the number of cubes to show the number of stickers, and then mark an X on the cube train that shows less stickers in number than the other cube train. Have them explain their cube trains.

Topic 2 | Lesson 6

Independent Practice

2

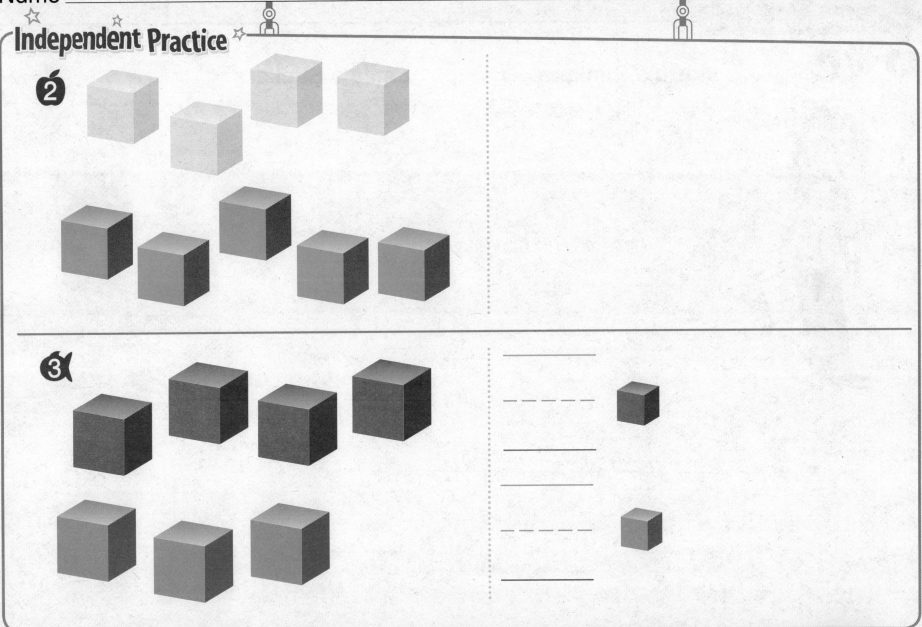

3

_____

_ _ _ _ _ _ _ _

_____

_____

_ _ _ _ _ _ _ _

_____

Directions **2** Say: *Carlos has 4 yellow blocks and 5 blue blocks. Which group of blocks is greater in number than the other group? How can you use a drawing to show your answer?* Have students create a drawing to show and explain their answer. **3** Say: *Carlos has 4 red blocks and 3 blue blocks. Which group of blocks is less in number than the other group? How can you use numbers to show your answer?* Have students use numbers to show and explain their answer.

Marta's Stickers

Emily's Stickers

Name _____

Another Look!

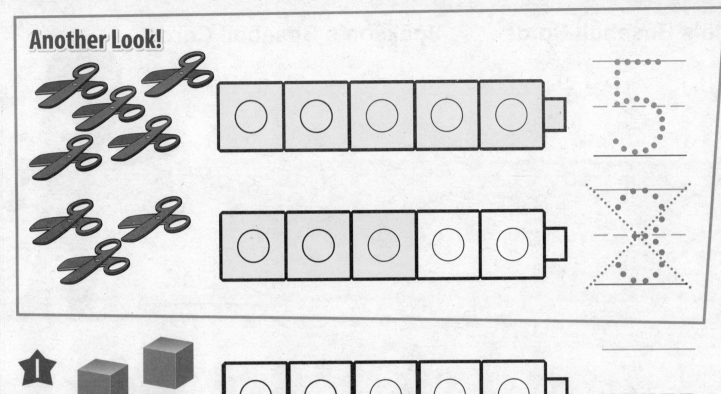

HOME ACTIVITY Make a group of 4 raisins or other small objects, and then write the number. Ask your child to make a group of 3 raisins or other small objects, and then write the number of raisins. Ask your child to use the numbers to explain which group is greater in number than the other group. Repeat with different numbers from 0 to 5.

⭐ 1

Directions Have students listen to the story. Say: *Mr. Davis has 5 blue scissors and 3 red scissors for his class. Which group of scissors has less than the other group? How can you use cubes, a drawing, or numbers to find out? Create cube or object trains for each group, color the number of cubes, and then write the numbers to tell how many. Mark an X on the number that is less than the other number.* Have students repeat the steps for this story: ⭐ *Candice has 4 purple blocks and 2 yellow blocks. Which group of blocks is less in number than the other group?*

Marta's Baseball Cards   Jackson's Baseball Cards

Directions Read the problem aloud. Then have students use multiple problem-solving methods to solve the problem. Say: *Marta has 5 baseball cards. Jackson has less in number than Marta does. How many baseball cards could Jackson have?* ❷ **Make Sense** *What do you know about the problem? What is the number of baseball cards Jackson CANNOT have? Tell a partner and explain why.*
❸ **Model** *Use cubes, draw a picture, or use numbers to show how many baseball cards Marta has and Jackson could have.*
❹ **Explain** *Tell a partner why your work for Jackson's baseball cards is correct.*

★

🍎 2

|

———————
– – – – – –
———————

◀ 3

● ●

♥ 4

Directions **Understand Vocabulary** Have students: ★ draw 5 counters in a **group**; 🍎 write the number that is **less than** the number shown; ◀ draw a group of counters that is **equal** in number to the group of counters shown; ♥ **compare** red and yellow counters using matching to find which group is less in number than the other, and then mark an X on that group.

5

6 4

_____
- - - - - - -
_____

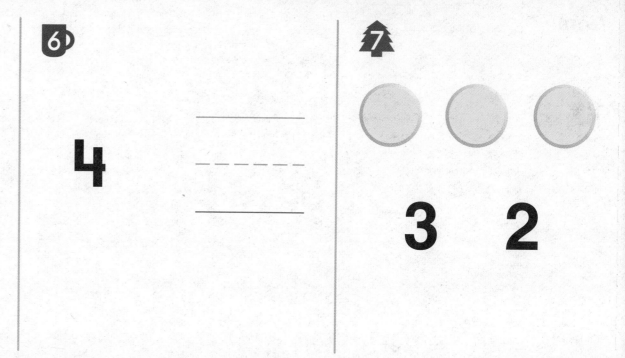

3   **2**

8

Topic 2 | Vocabulary Review

Name _____

Set A

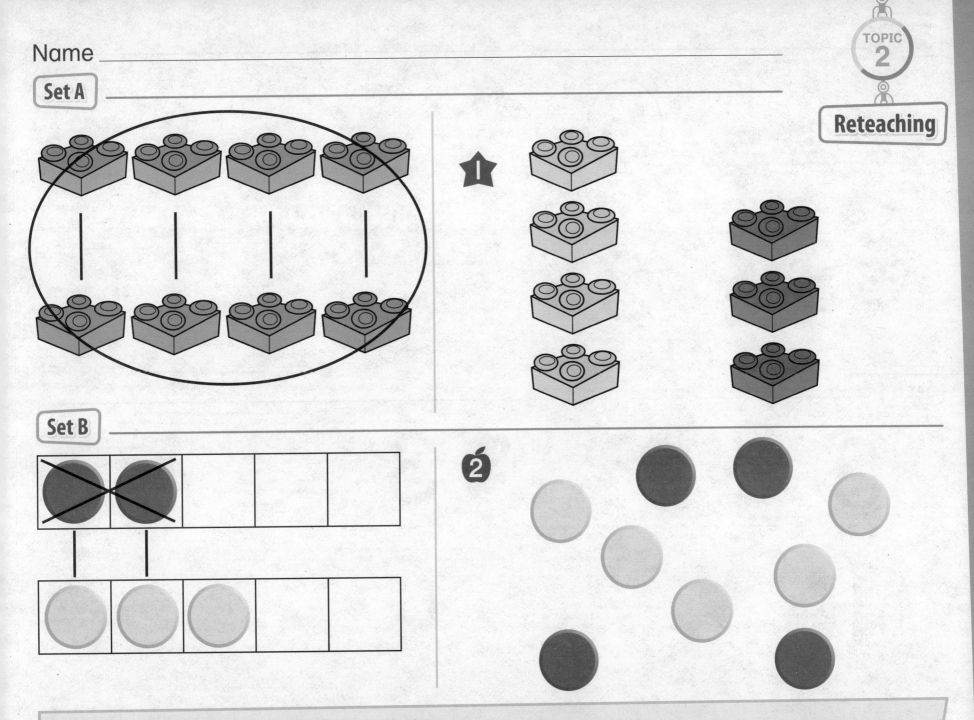

★

Set B

❷

Directions Have students: ★ draw lines between the rows to match the blocks from one group to the other group. Then have them draw a circle around the groups if they are equal, or mark an X on the groups if they are NOT equal; ❷ draw lines to match the groups of red and yellow counters. Have them draw a circle around the group that is greater in number than the other group, and then explain why they are correct.

Directions Have students: 🐿 count the stickers, and then draw a circle around the number that is greater than the other number and mark an X on the number that is less than the other number; 🍌 draw a circle around the number that is greater than the other number, or draw a circle around both numbers if they are equal. Have students draw pictures to show how they know.

Name _____

Ⓐ

Ⓑ

Ⓒ

Ⓓ

☐

☐

☐

☐

❸

4

4

Directions ⭐ Which group of tennis balls is greater in number than the group of baseballs? ❷ Mark all the groups of red counters that are NOT equal in number to the group of yellow counters. ❸ Have students draw a circle around the number that is greater than the other number, or draw a circle around both numbers if they are equal. Then have students draw pictures to show how they know.

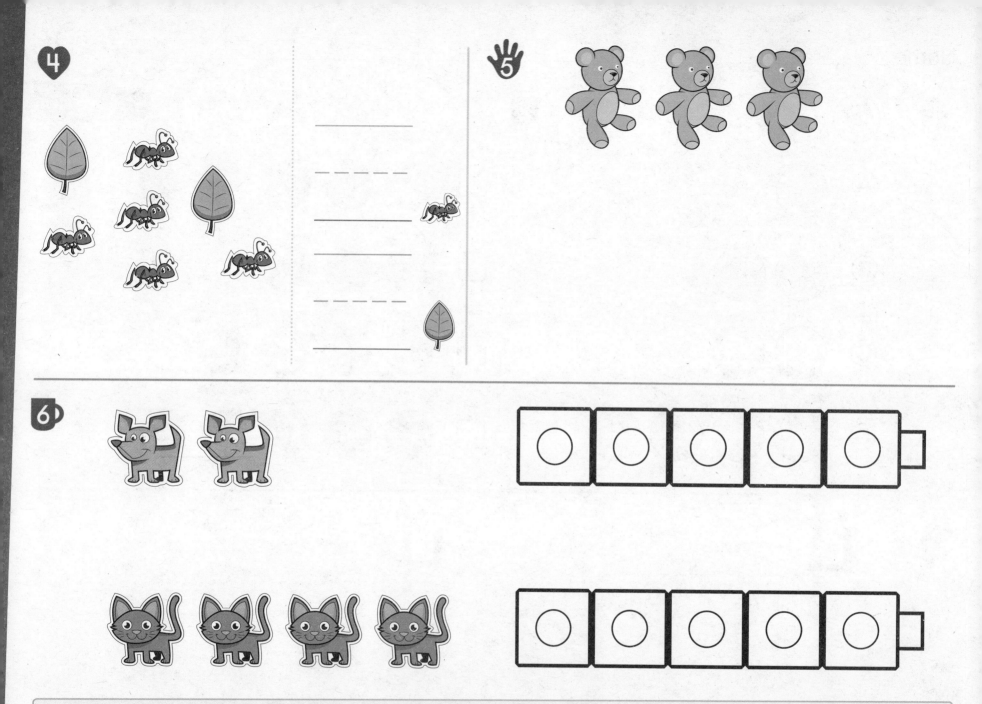

Name _____

⭐ 1

_____

- - - - - - - -

_____

- - - - - - - -

_____

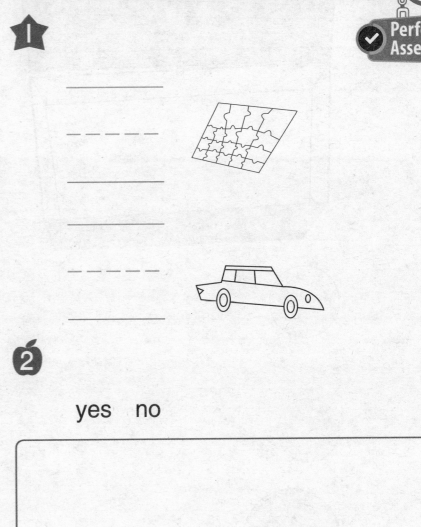

🍎 2

yes   no

[ ]

Directions **Toy Chest** Say: *David keeps his toys in a toy chest.* ⭐ Have students count the jigsaw puzzles and cars that David can see in the toy chest, and then write the numbers to tell how many. Then have them draw a circle around the number that is greater than the other number and mark an X on the number that is less than the other number. 🍎 Say: *David says that his group of toy cars is greater than his group of alphabet blocks. Do you agree with him?* Have students draw a circle around **yes** or **no**, and then have them draw a picture to explain their answer.

3

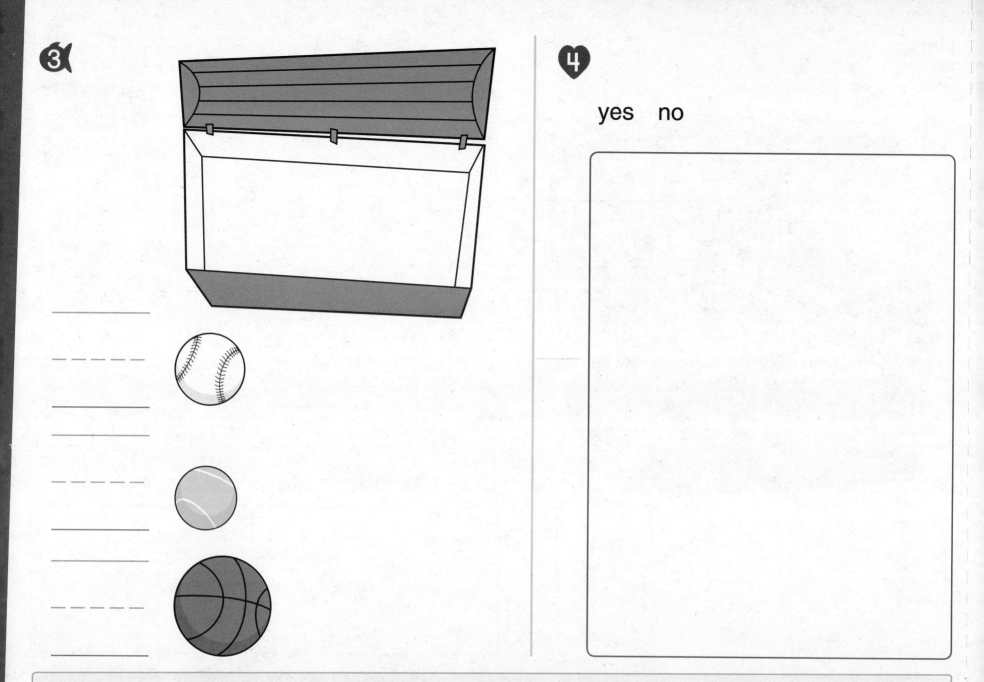

_____

- - - - - - - -

_____

_____

- - - - - - - -

4 ♥

yes   no

Topic 2 | Performance Assessment

Numbers 6 to 10

Essential Question: How can numbers from 6 to 10 be counted, read, and written?

Digital Resources

Solve · Learn · Glossary

Tools · Assessment · Help · Games

Rain showers

Weather can be good and bad.

Math and Science Project: Types of Weather

Directions Read the character speech bubbles to students. **Find Out!** Have students discuss different types of weather they have experienced. Say: *Talk to friends and relatives about weather. Ask which types of weather they have seen.* **Journal: Make a Poster** Have students make a poster. Have them draw 10 pictures to represent good and bad weather they have experienced. Ask them to sort their pictures into two groups that show types of weather they enjoy and types they do not enjoy. Have students count how many are in each group and write the numbers.

Name _____

 1

 2

4

5

3

4

5

_____

- - - - - - -

_____

- - - - - - -

Directions Have students: ⭐ draw a circle around the group that is greater in number than the other group; 🍎 mark an X on the number that is less than the other number; 🌀 mark an X on the group that is less in number than the other group; ♥ count the objects, write the number to tell how many of each, and then draw a circle around the number that is greater than the other number; ✋ draw a group of counters that is equal in number to the group of counters shown.

My Word Cards

Directions Have students cut out the vocabulary cards. Read the front of the card, and then ask them to explain what the word or phrase means.

A-Z
Glossary

six

seven

eight

nine

ten

My Word Cards

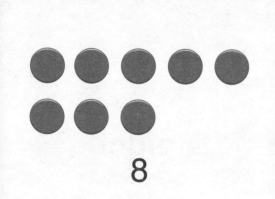

8

Point to the picture.
Say: *This is the number* **eight**.

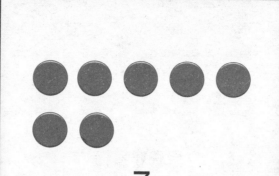

7

Point to the picture.
Say: *This is the number* **seven**.

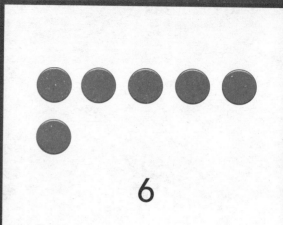

6

Point to the picture.
Say: *This is the number* **six**.

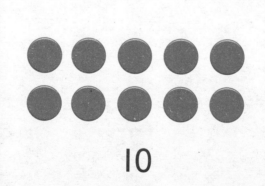

10

Point to the picture.
Say: *This is the number* **ten**.

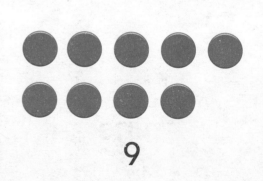

9

Point to the picture.
Say: *This is the number* **nine**.

Name _____

Solve

Lesson 3-1
Count 6 and 7

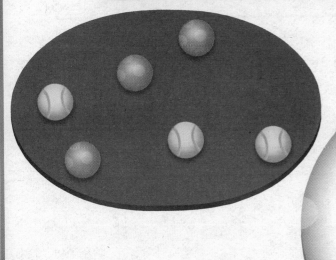

Directions Say: *Jackson's dog, Rex, has some balls on the red rug. Use counters and draw a picture on the empty dog bed to show how many balls Rex has. Tell how you know you are correct.*

I can ...
count the numbers 6 and 7.

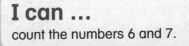

I can also use math tools correctly.

☆ Guided Practice

1

2

Directions ⭐ and ➋ Have students draw a counter as they count each dog to show how many.

140 one hundred forty

Topic 3 | Lesson I

Name _____

Directions ★–✋ Have students draw a counter as they count each animal to show how many.

Topic 3 | Lesson 1

one hundred forty-one   141

Independent Practice

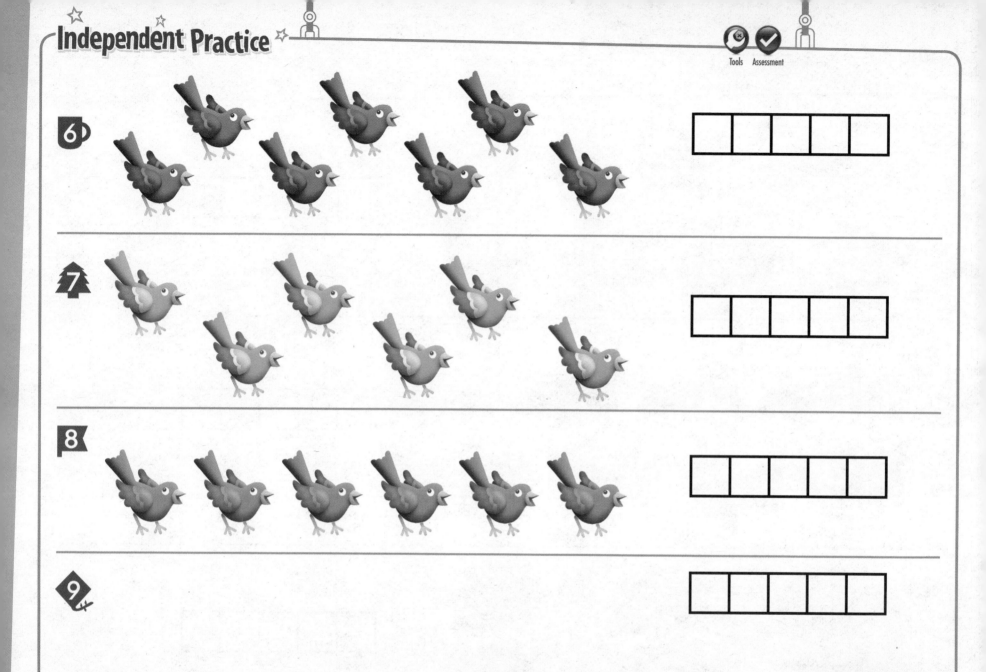

6

7

8

9

Directions 6–8 Have students draw a counter as they count each bird to show how many. ❷ **Higher Order Thinking** Have students draw 6 or 7 eggs, and then draw a counter as they draw each egg to show how many.

Topic 3 | Lesson 1

Name _____

Another Look!

HOME ACTIVITY Have your child count groups of 6 objects. Then have him or her draw pictures of 6 objects. Repeat using the number 7.

⭐ 1

2

3

Directions Say: *Count the dots and put down a counter or other object for each number you count. Then draw counters in the box to show the same number of counters as dots.* ⭐–❸ *Have students count the number of dots, place a counter or other object for each dot they count, and then draw counters in the box to show the same number of counters as dots.*

Topic 3 | Lesson 1

4

5

6

Directions ♥ **Math and Science** Ask students why a rain shower would be good for flowers. Have students draw a counter as they count each flower to show how many. ✋ **Higher Order Thinking** Have students draw a circle around the same number of flowers as counters. ☕ **Higher Order Thinking** Have students color red the vase with 6 flowers, and then color yellow the vase with 7 flowers.

Topic 3 | Lesson 1

Solve & Share

Directions   Say: *Jackson sees 7 beach balls. How can he show how many beach balls in two different ways? Draw the ways on the blankets.*

I can ...
read and write the numbers
6 and 7.

I can also make math arguments.

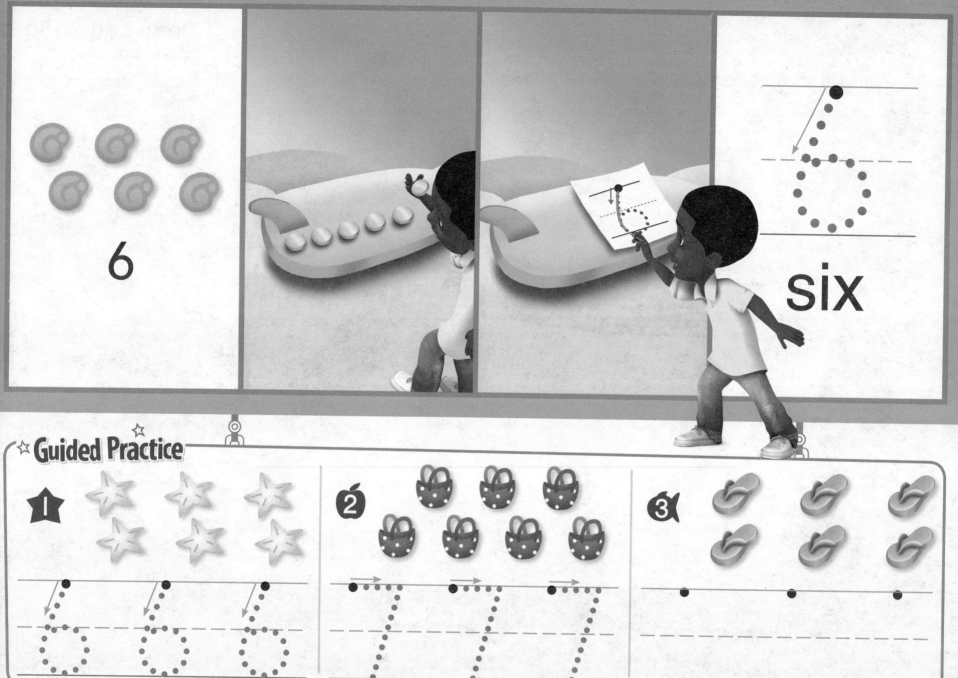

6

six

☆ Guided Practice

1

2

3

Directions **1**–**3** Have students count the objects, and then practice writing the number that tells how many.

Topic 3 | Lesson 2

Name _____

4 ♥

5 ✋

6 ☕

7 🌲

Directions ♥–🌲 Have students count the objects, and then practice writing the number that tells how many.

Topic 3 | Lesson 2

one hundred forty-seven **147**

Independent Practice

8 _____

_____

_____

9 _____

_____

_____

10

Directions **8** and **9** Have students count the fish, and then practice writing the number that tells how many.
10 **Higher Order Thinking** Have students count each group of objects, and then write the numbers to tell how many.

148 one hundred forty-eight   Copyright © Savvas Learning Company LLC. All Rights Reserved.   **Topic 3** | Lesson 2

Name ______________________

Help Tools Games

Homework & Practice 3-2

Read and Write 6 and 7

HOME ACTIVITY Draw groups of 6 and 7 circles on 2 index cards. Have your child write the correct number on the back of each card. Then use the cards to practice counting and reading the numbers 6 and 7.

Another Look!

6 6 6

7 7 7

1

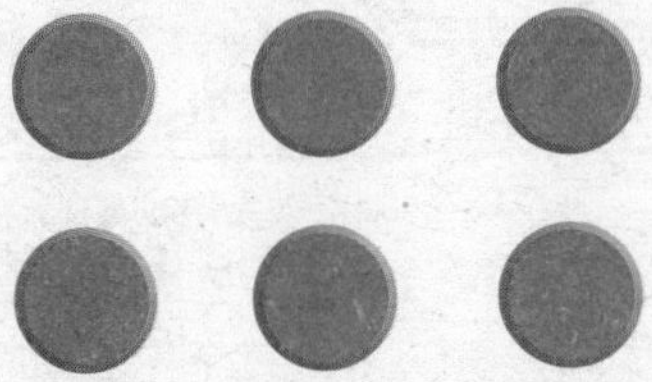

2

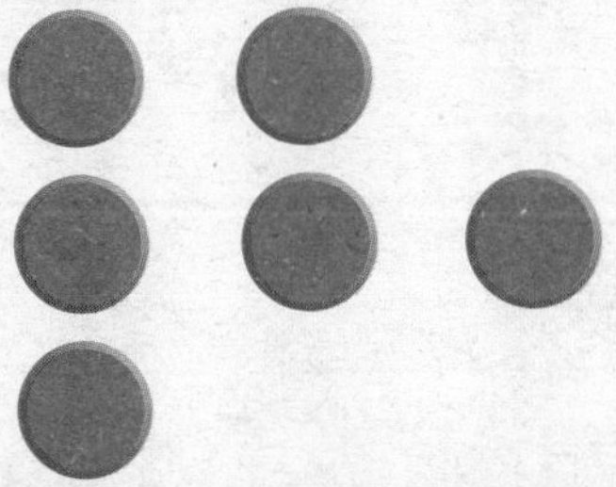

3

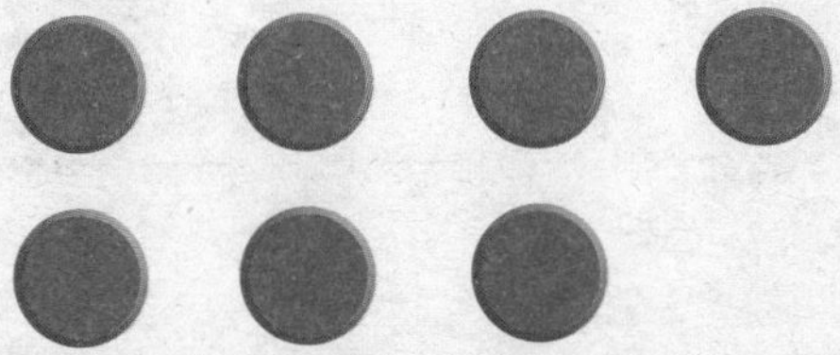

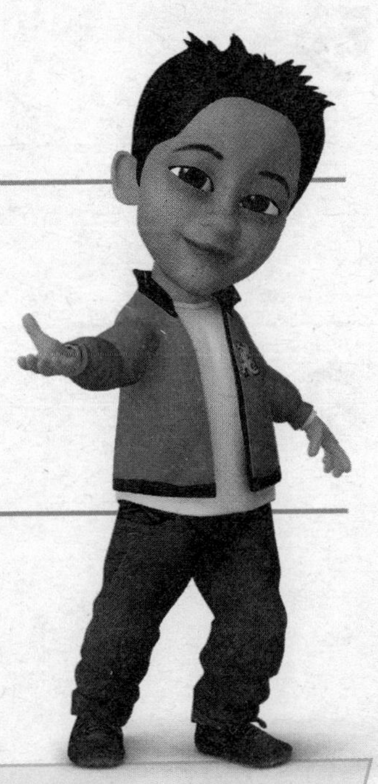

Directions Say: *Count the counters, and then practice writing the numbers that tell how many.* 1–3 Have students count the counters, and then practice writing the number that tells how many.

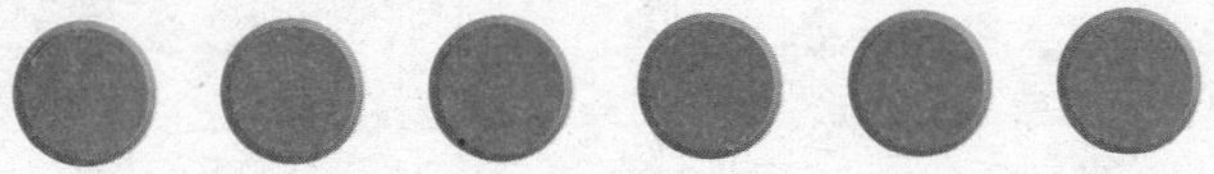

4 _____

5 _____

6 _____

7 _____

Directions ♥ and ✋ Have students count the objects, and then practice writing the number that tells how many. ☕ **Higher Order Thinking** Have students draw more beach balls to show 7, and then practice writing the number 7. 🌲 **Higher Order Thinking** Have students draw 6 or 7 fish, and then practice writing the number that tells how many.

Name _____

Directions Say: *Jackson makes some sandwiches for lunch at the beach. Use counters and draw a picture on the blank sign to show how many sandwiches Jackson makes. Tell how you know you are correct.*

I can ... count the numbers 8 and 9.

I can also model with math.

Topic 3 | Lesson 3
Digital Resources at SavvasRealize.com
one hundred fifty-one **151**

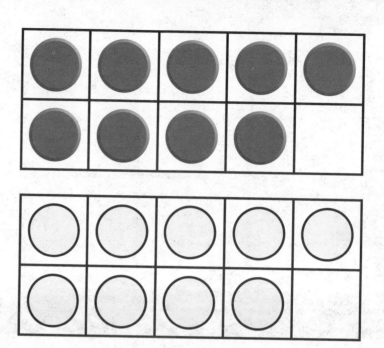

☆ Guided Practice

1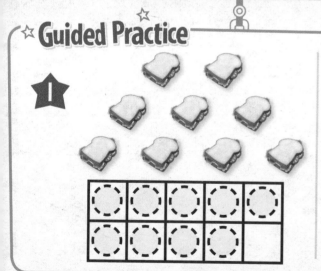

2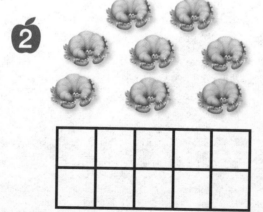

3

Directions ⭐–❸ Have students count the sandwiches, and then draw counters to show how many.

152   one hundred fifty-two

Name _____

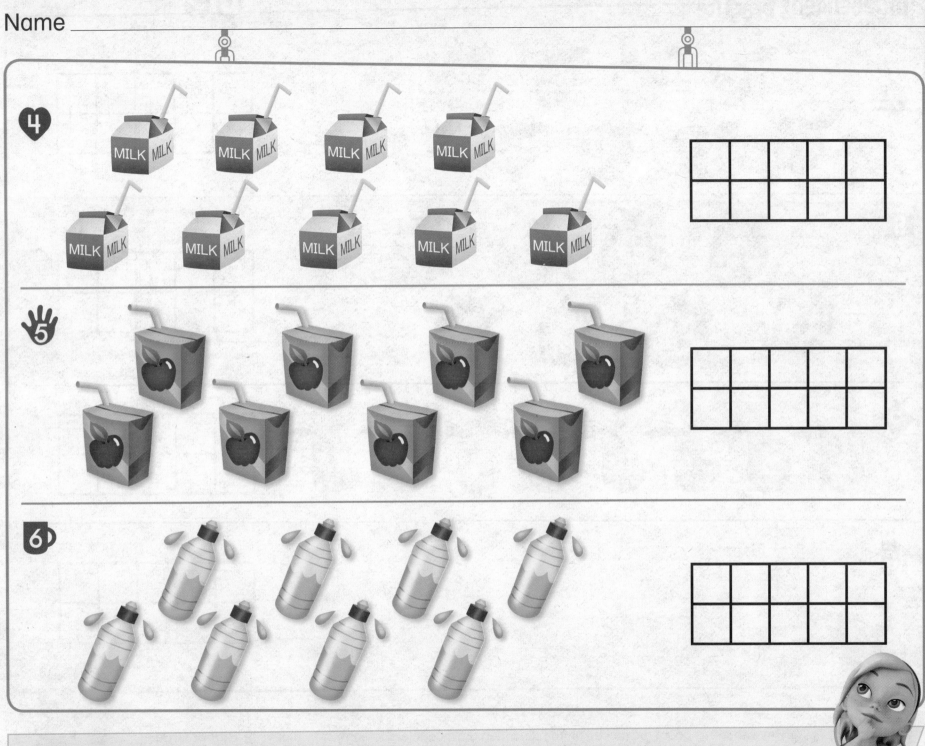

Directions ❤️–🍵 Have students count the drinks, and then draw counters to show how many.

Topic 3 | Lesson 3   one hundred fifty-three   153

Independent Practice

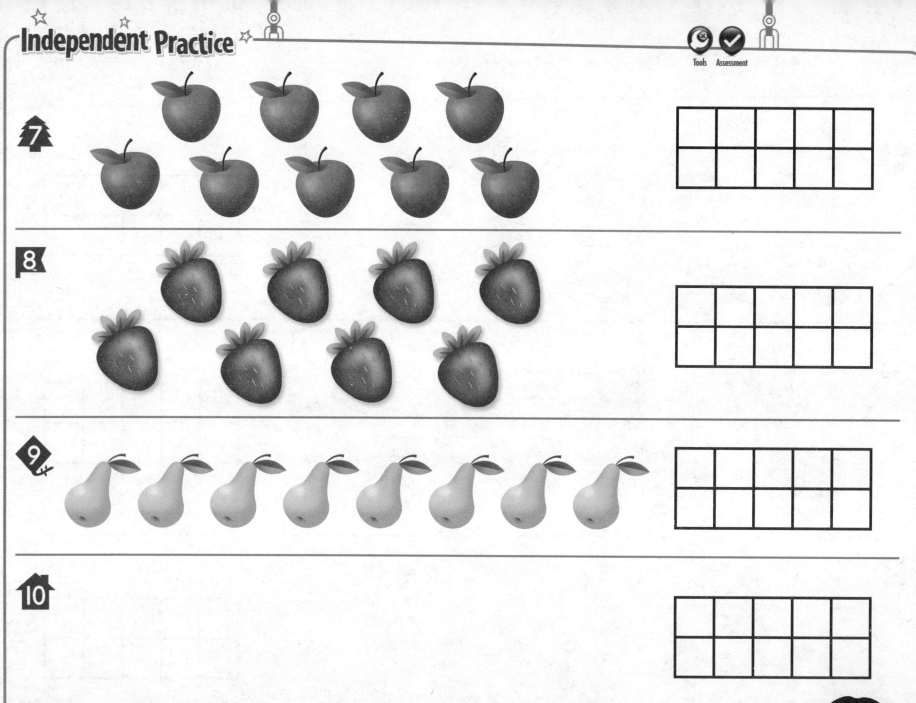

7

8

9

10

Topic 3 | **Lesson 3**

Name _____

Another Look!

HOME ACTIVITY Have your child count groups of 8 objects. Then ask him or her to draw pictures of 8 objects. Repeat using the number 9.

⭐1

2

3

Directions Say: *Count the dots and use counters or other objects to show that number. Then draw counters in the box to show the same number of counters as dots.* ⭐—3 Have students count the number of dots, use counters or other objects to show that number, and then draw counters in the box to show the same number of counters as dots.

Directions ❹ Have students count the sandwiches, and then draw counters to show how many. ✋ **Higher Order Thinking** Have students draw a circle around the same number of sandwiches as counters. ❻ **Higher Order Thinking** Have students color brown the dog with 8 spots, and then color black the dog with 9 spots.

Topic 3 | Lesson 3

Solve & Share

Name _____

I can ...
read and write the numbers
8 and 9.

I can also make math
arguments.

Directions Say: *Jackson sees 9 turtle eggs in the sand. How can he show how many turtle eggs in two different ways? Draw the ways on the turtle shells.*

8

eight

☆ Guided Practice

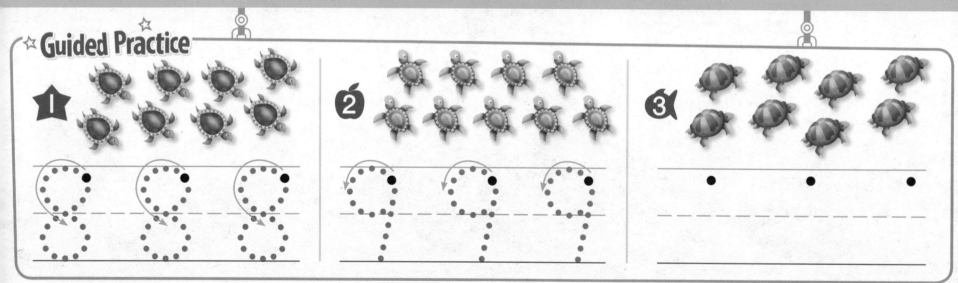

1

2

3

Directions ⭐–🐬 Have students count the turtles, and then practice writing the number that tells how many.

Name _____

Directions ♥–🌲 Have students count the animals, and then practice writing the number that tells how many.

Topic 3 | Lesson 4

one hundred fifty-nine **159**

Independent Practice

8

_____

_____

9

_____

_____

10 _____

_____

_____

Directions **8** and **9** Have students count the animals, and then practice writing the number that tells how many.
10 **Higher Order Thinking** Have students count each group of animals, and then write the numbers that tell how many.

Name _____

Another Look!

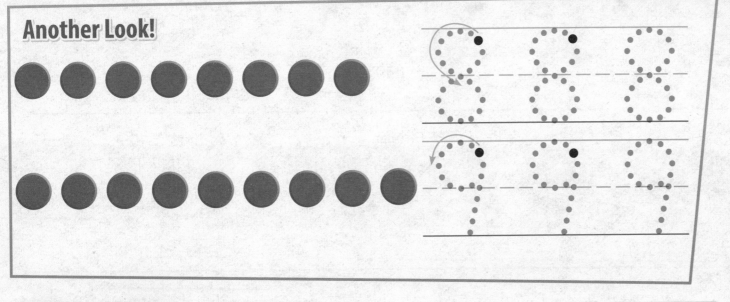

HOME ACTIVITY Draw groups of 8 and 9 circles on 2 index cards. Have your child write the correct number on the back of each card. Then use the cards to practice counting and reading the numbers 8 and 9.

Directions Say: *Count the counters, and then practice writing the number that tells how many.* ★–❸ Have students count the dots, and then practice writing the number that tells how many.

4 ❤

(dolphins)

_____

- - - - - - - - - - - -

_____

5 ✋

(seahorses)

_____

- - - - - - - - - - - -

_____

6 ☕

(beach balls)

_____

- - - - - - - - - - - -

_____

7 🌲

_____

- - - - - - - - - - - -

_____

Directions 4 and 5 Have students count the animals, and then practice writing the number that tells how many. 6 **Higher Order Thinking** Have students draw more beach balls to show 9, and then practice writing the number 9. 7 **Higher Order Thinking** Have students draw 8 or 9 fish, and then practice writing the number that tells how many.

Solve & Share

Name _____

Solve

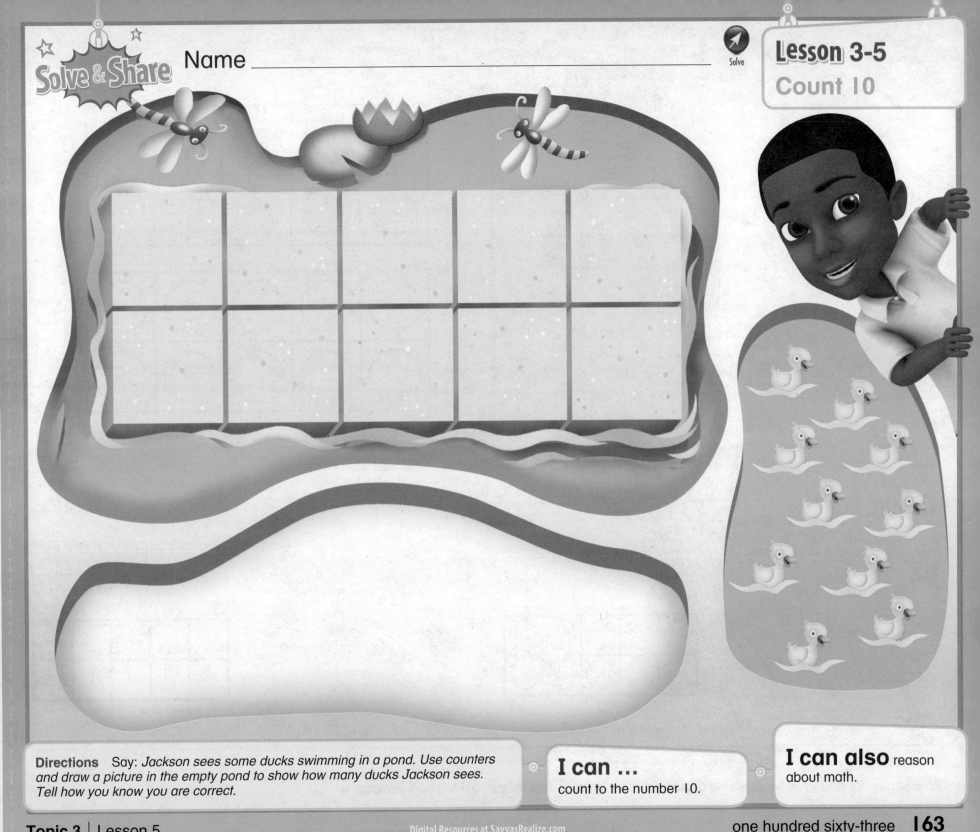

Directions Say: *Jackson sees some ducks swimming in a pond. Use counters and draw a picture in the empty pond to show how many ducks Jackson sees. Tell how you know you are correct.*

I can ... count to the number 10.

I can also reason about math.

☆ Guided Practice

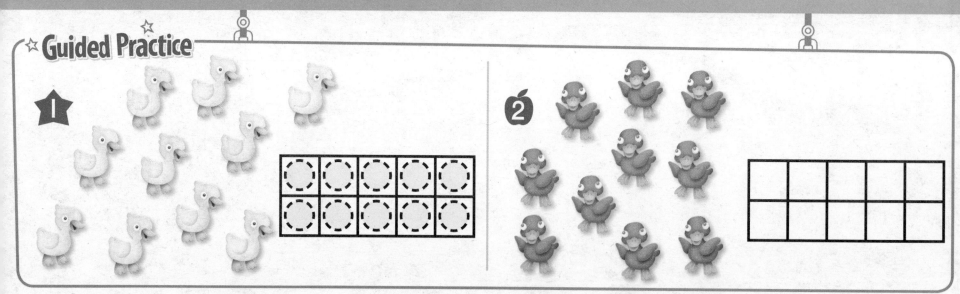

Directions ⭐ and ② Have students draw a counter for each bird they count to show how many.

Topic 3 | **Lesson 5**

Name _____

3

4

Directions **3** and **4** Have students draw a counter for each bird they count to show how many.

Topic 3 | Lesson 5

one hundred sixty-five **165**

Independent Practice

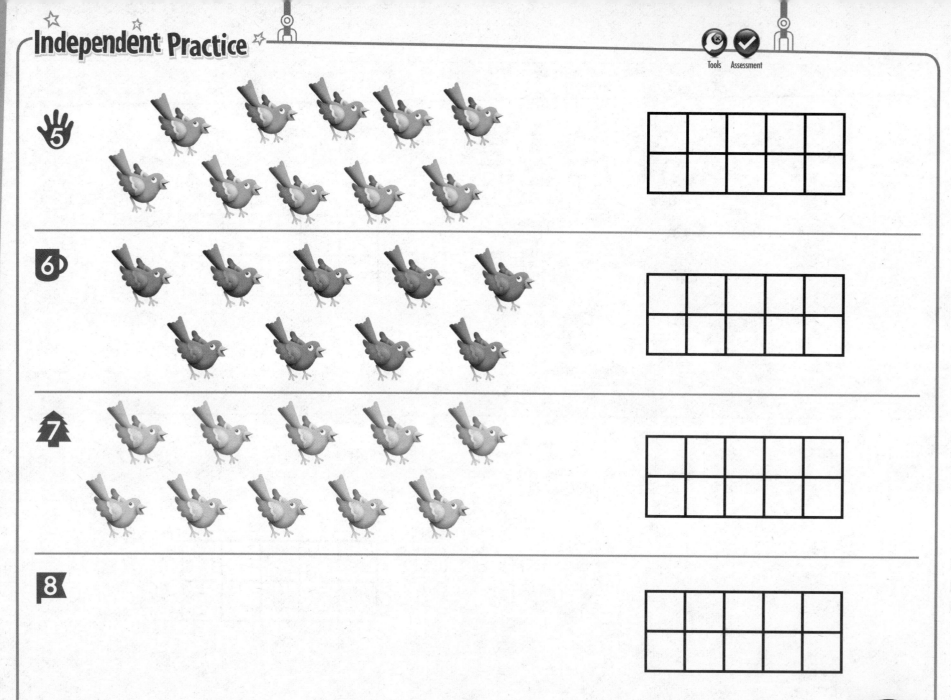

166 one hundred sixty-six

Topic 3 | Lesson 5

Name _____

Homework & Practice 3-5
Count 10

Another Look!

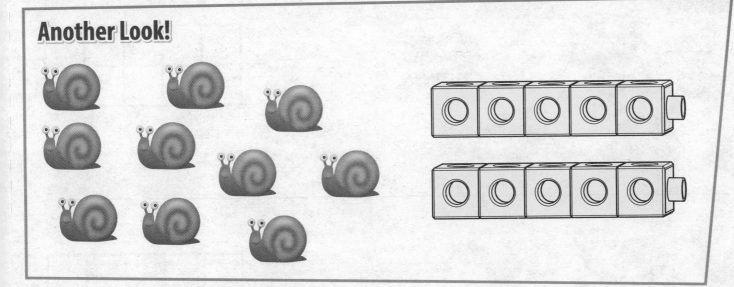

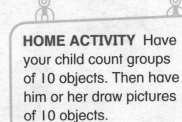

HOME ACTIVITY Have your child count groups of 10 objects. Then have him or her draw pictures of 10 objects.

⭐ 1

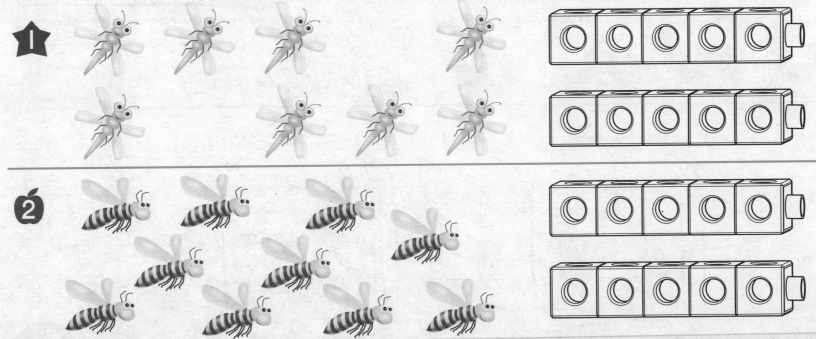

🍎 2

Directions Say: *Count the snails and use connecting cubes or other objects to show that number. Then color a connecting cube for each snail you counted to show the same number of cubes as snails.* ⭐ and 🍎 *Have students count the insects, use connecting cubes or other objects to show that number, and then color a connecting cube for each insect they count to show the same number of cubes as insects.*

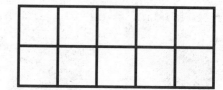

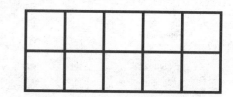

Directions ❸ Have students count the ladybugs, and then draw counters to show how many. ❹ **Higher Order Thinking** Have students draw more worms to show 10, and then draw counters to show how many. ✋ **Higher Order Thinking** Have students look at the jars, color red the jar with 9 fireflies, and then color yellow the jar with 10 fireflies.

168 one hundred sixty-eight

Topic 3 | Lesson 5

Solve & Share

Name _____

Solve

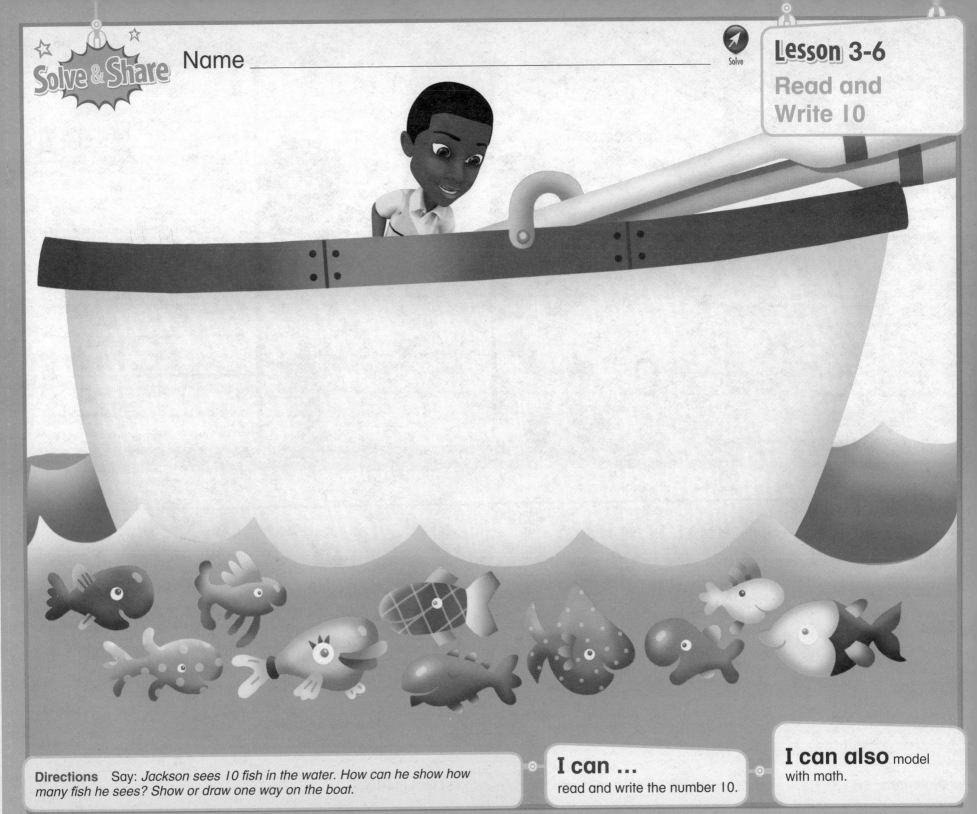

Directions Say: *Jackson sees 10 fish in the water. How can he show how many fish he sees? Show or draw one way on the boat.*

I can …
read and write the number 10.

I can also model
with math.

10

10

ten

☆ Guided Practice

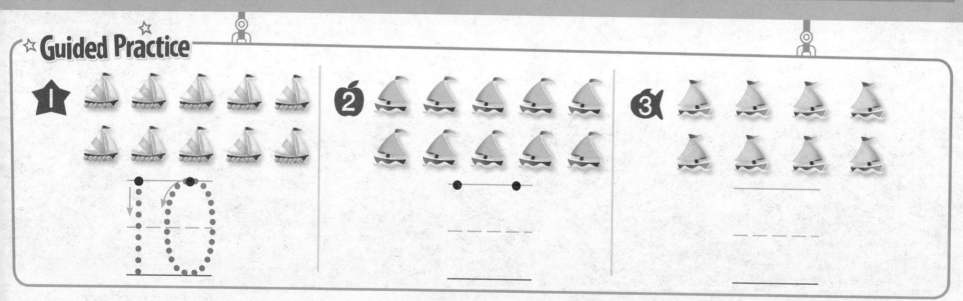

1

2

3

Directions 1–3 Have students count the boats, and then write the number to tell how many.

Name _____

4

_____
- - - - - - - - -
_____

5

_____
- - - - - - - - -
_____

6

_____
- - - - - - - - -
_____

Directions **4**–**6** Have students count the boats, and then write the number to tell how many.

Topic 3 | Lesson 6

one hundred seventy-one **171**

Independent Practice

🌲7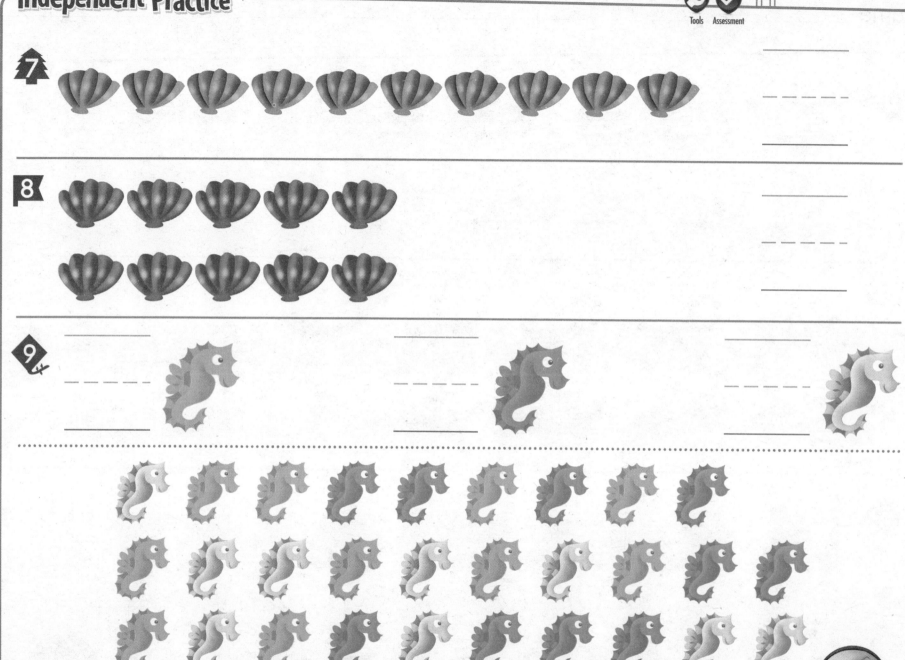

_____

- - - - -

_____

8

_____

- - - - -

_____

9

- - - - - _____

- - - - -

- - - - - _____

172 one hundred seventy-two

Name _____

Another Look!

HOME ACTIVITY Draw groups of 9 and 10 circles on 2 index cards. Have your child write the correct number on the back of each card. Then use the cards to practice counting and reading the numbers 9 and 10.

_____

- - - - - - -

_____

- - - - - - -

_____

- - - - - - -

Directions Say: *Count the sea stars, and then write the number to tell how many.* ⭐ Have students count each group of sea stars, and then write the number to tell how many.

2

3

4

5

174 one hundred seventy-four

Topic 3 | Lesson 6

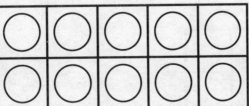

Directions Say: *Jackson puts 10 watering cans on a shelf in the garden store. How can you use counters to show the 10 watering cans in a different way? Color the counters red and yellow to show your work.*

I can ... show how to make a group of 10.

I can also reason about math.

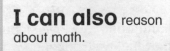

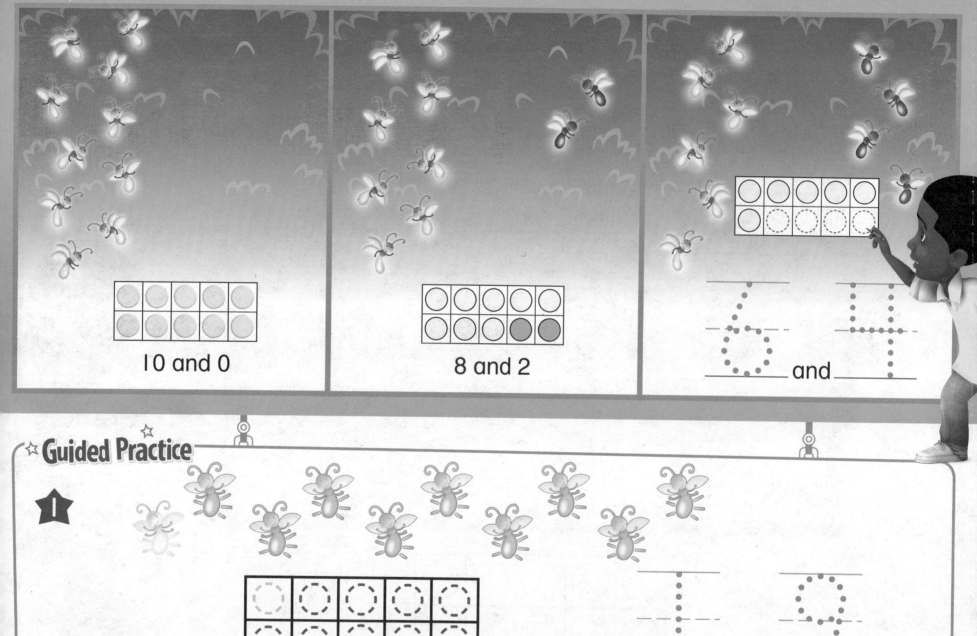

10 and 0

8 and 2

_____ and _____

☆ Guided Practice

1

_____ and _____

Directions ★ Have students draw and color counters red and yellow to show one way to make 10, color the fireflies red and yellow to show that way, and then write the numbers.

176 one hundred seventy-six

Topic 3 | Lesson 7

Name_____

2

_____ _____

_____ and _____

3

_____ _____

_____ and _____

4

_____ _____

_____ and _____

Directions ❷–❹ Have students draw and color counters red and yellow to show one way to make 10, color the insects red and yellow to show each way, and then write the numbers.

Independent Practice

5

_____ and _____

_____ and _____

6

_____ and _____

_____ and _____

7

_____ and _____

_____ and _____

Directions 👋 and **6** Have students draw and color counters red and yellow to show one way to make 10, color the insects red and yellow to show each way, and then write the numbers. **7** **Higher Order Thinking** Have students draw a way to make 10, and then write the numbers.

Topic 3 | Lesson 7

Name _____

Help Tools Games

Homework & Practice 3-7

Ways to Make 10

Another Look!

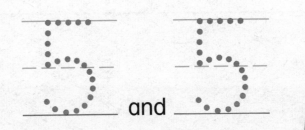

_5_ and _5_

HOME ACTIVITY Have your child show the number 10 in different ways using 10 cards or pictures. Ask your child to tell the two parts that make the 10. Have your child show one part of the 10 pictures or cards facedown and the other part faceup.

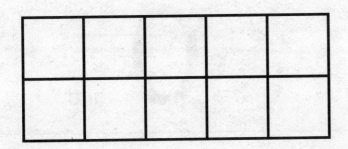

_____ _____

_ _ _ _ _ _   _ _ _ _ _ _

_____ and _____

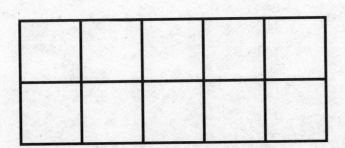

_____ _____

_ _ _ _ _ _   _ _ _ _ _ _

_____ and _____

Directions Say: *Use red and blue cubes or pieces of paper to model this way to make 10, and then write the numbers.* ⭐ and
② **Vocabulary** Have students use red and blue cubes or pieces of paper to find two different ways to make **ten**, draw the cubes to show each way, and then write the numbers.

3 🪣🪣🪣🪣

_____
4 and _ _ _ _ _

4 🧤🧤🧤

_____
3 and _ _ _ _ _

5 ✋

_____
0 and _____

6

_____   _____
_ _ _ _   _ _ _ _ | _ _ _ _   _ _ _ _
_____ and _____ | _____ and _____

180 one hundred eighty

Topic 3 | Lesson 7

Name _____

Solve

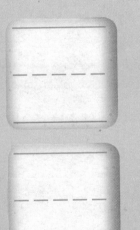

Think.

Directions Say: *Jackson decorates his sand castle with 3 shells. He has two different colors of shells. He wants to show all the ways to decorate his sand castle with 3 shells. How can he use a pattern to show all the ways to make 3?*

I can ...
use counting patterns to solve a problem.

I can also count to 10.

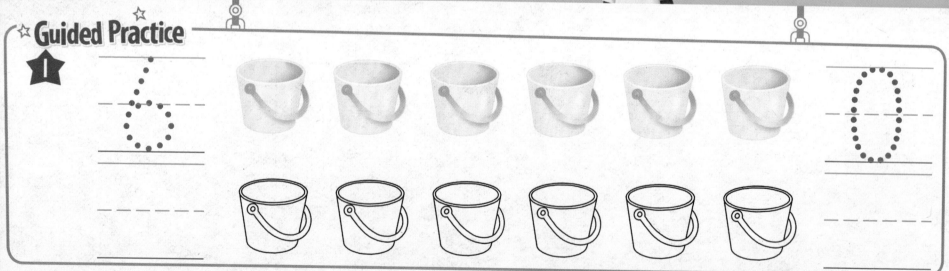

Guided Practice

⭐1

Directions Say: *How can you color the pails to show different ways to make 6?* 🔺 Have students use red and yellow crayons to make a pattern showing two ways to make 6, and then write the numbers. Have them describe the pattern.

Topic 3 | Lesson 8

Independent Practice

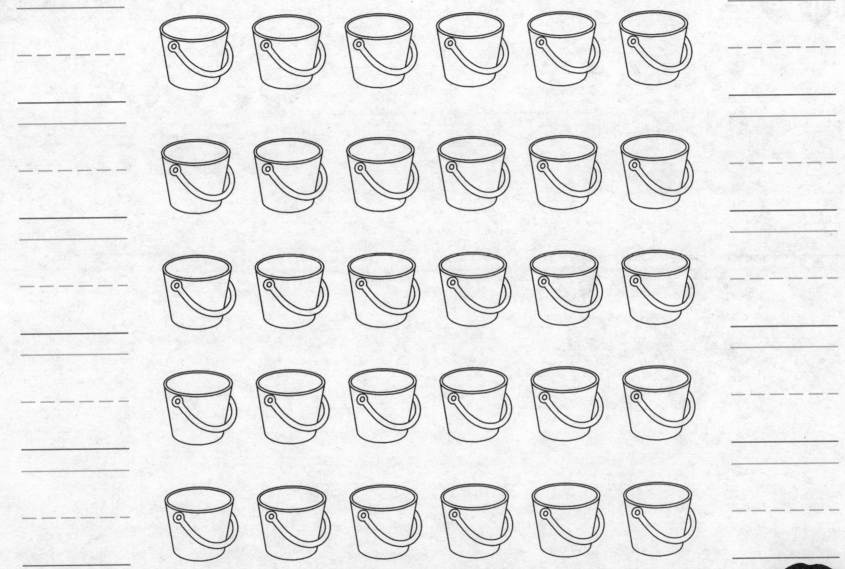

Directions Say: *How can you color the pails to show different ways to make 6?* ❷ Have students look at Items 1 and 2, and then use red and yellow crayons to complete the pattern showing five ways to make 6. Then have them write the numbers, and then describe the pattern.

Problem Solving

③ ④ ✋

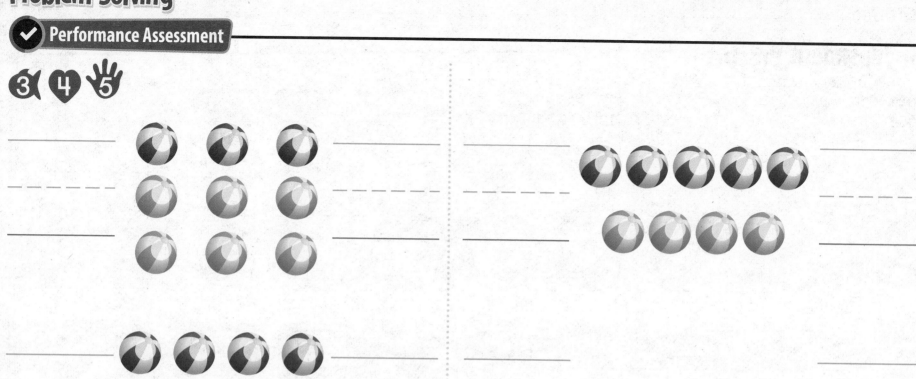

Directions Read the problem to students. Then have them use multiple problem-solving methods to solve the problem. Say: *Mr. Sand runs a game at the beach. The prizes are red and blue beach balls. He displays them in a pattern. What is the next row in the pattern?* ③ **Use Tools** *What tool can you use to help solve the problem?* ④ **Generalize** *How can the ways that are shown help you find the next way to make 9?* ✋ **Look for Patterns** *What is the next way in the pattern to make 9? Write the numbers for that way.*

Name _____

2

_____
_ _ _ _ _
_____
_ _ _ _ _
_____

3

_____
_ _ _ _ _
_____
_____
_ _ _ _ _
_____

Directions **2** Have students count the vegetables in each group, write the number to tell how many, draw a line from each vegetable in the top group to a vegetable in the bottom group, and then mark an X on the number that is less than the other number. **3 Number Sense** Have students count the vegetables in each group, draw more pea pods to make the groups equal, write the numbers to tell how many in each group, and then draw a line from each vegetable in the top group to a vegetable in the bottom group to compare.

Independent Practice

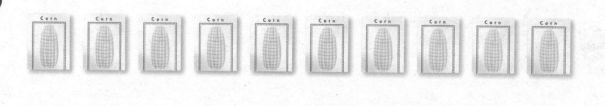

_____

- - - - - - -

_____

_____

- - - - - - -

_____

_____

- - - - - - -

_____

_____

- - - - - - -

_____

Directions ♥ Have students count the seed packets in each group, write the number to tell how many, draw a line from each seed packet in the top group to a seed packet in the bottom group, and then mark an X on the number that is less than the other number. ✋ **Higher Order Thinking** Have students count the flowers in the group, draw a group of flowers that is less than the group shown, and then write the numbers to tell how many.

       Topic 4 | Lesson 2

Name _____

Another Look!

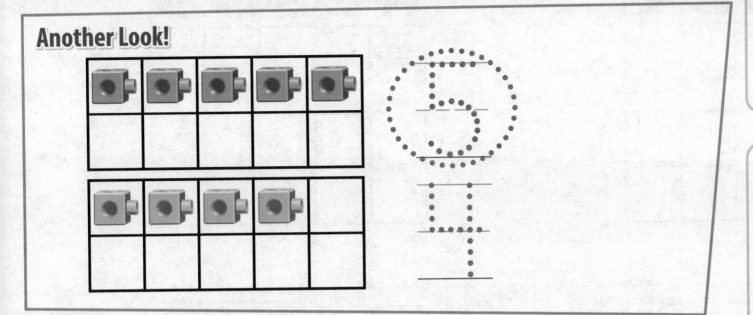

HOME ACTIVITY Show a group of up to 10 objects, such as buttons. Ask your child to show a group of objects that is greater in number than your group. Repeat with a group that is less in number than your group of objects.

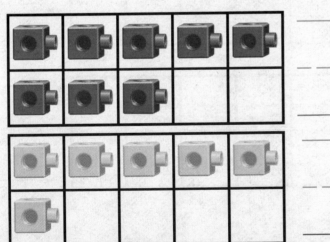

Directions Say: *Count the cubes in each group, write the number to tell how many, and then draw a circle around the number that is greater than the other number.* ⭐ and ❷ Have students count the cubes in each group, write the number to tell how many, and then mark an X on the number that is less than the other number.

Topic 4 | Lesson 2
Digital Resources at SavvasRealize.com
two hundred eleven **211**

Name _____

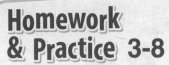
Another Look!

HOME ACTIVITY Place
10 crayons in a row across
a table (pointing upward).
Ask your child to show a
way to make 10 by pointing
1 crayon down. Ask your
child to write the numbers
for the two groups (1 and 9).
Then have your child use
the crayons to show all the
other ways to make 10 and
then write the numbers.

Directions Say: *You can make a pattern to show all of the different ways to make 4. First, you can color to show 0 red shells and 4 yellow shells. Next, you can color to show 1 red shell and 3 yellow shells. Write the numbers.* 🟊 Say: *Show three other ways to make 4.* Have students color the shells red and yellow to complete the pattern showing all the ways to make 4, and then write the numbers. Have them describe the pattern.

Directions Read the problem to students. Then have them use multiple problem-solving methods to solve the problem. Say: *Elijah has red and yellow napkins. He must set out napkins for 4 people. What are all the ways to make 4?* ❷ **Make Sense** *What is a good plan for solving the problem?* ❸ **Look for and Make Use of Structure** *What are all the ways to make 4? Write the ways on the lines at the top of the page.* ❹ **Reasoning** *How do you know that you have found all of the ways to make 4?*

Name _____

1

_____

- - - - - - - -

_____

2

8   9

3

5   - - - - - -   7

_____

4

_____   _____

- - - - - - -   - - - - - - -

_____   _____

Directions **Understand Vocabulary** Have students: **1** write the number **eight**; **2** draw a circle around the number **nine**; **3** write the missing number and then say it aloud; **4** write the parts that make 10.

5

10   9

 6

_____

- - - - - - - - - -

_____

 **7**

_____

- - - - - - - - - -

_____

8

_____   _____   _____   _____   _____

- - - - - - - - -   - - - - - - - - -   - - - - - - - - -   - - - - - - - - -   - - - - - - - - -

_____   _____   _____   _____   _____

- - - - - - - - -   - - - - - - - - -   - - - - - - - - -   - - - - - - - - -   - - - - - - - - -

_____   _____   _____   _____   _____

Directions **Understand Vocabulary** Have students: draw a circle around the number **ten**; write the number **seven**;  count the number of cubes, and then write the number to tell how many; **8** write numbers 1 to10 in order.

 Topic 3 | Vocabulary Review

Name _____

Set A

6

7

⭐

_____

- - - - - - - - - -

_____

🍎 ②

_____

- - - - - - - - - -

_____

Set B

⭐ ③

❤ ④

Directions Have students: ⭐ and ② count the objects, and then write the numbers to tell how many; ③ and ④ count the number of dots, place a counter for each dot they count, and then draw counters in the box to show the same number of counters as dots in a different way.

Set C

 8

 9

_____
- - - - - - - - - - -
_____

_____
- - - - - - - - - - -
_____

Set D

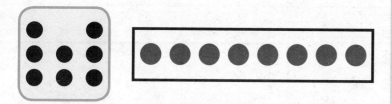

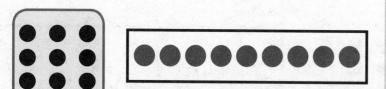

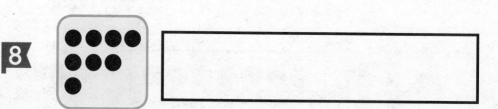

Directions Have students: 👋 and ☕ count the objects, and then write the number to tell how many; 🌲 and 🚩 count the number of dots, place a counter as they count each dot, and then draw counters in the box to show the same number of counters as dots in a different way.

Name _____

_____

9

Set F

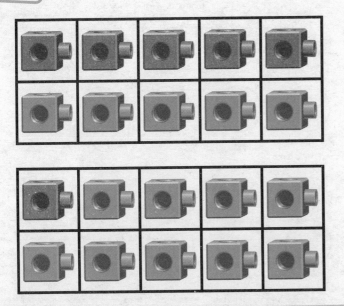

Directions Have students: 🐠 count the objects, and then practice writing the number that tells how many; 🏠 and 🌸 color the connecting cubes red and blue to show two different ways to make 10.

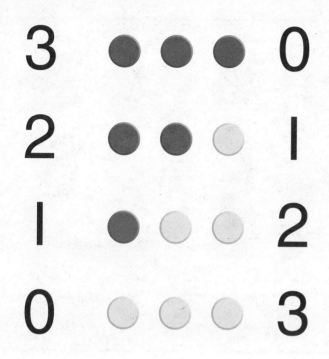

3 ● ● ●   0

2 ● ● ○   1

1 ● ○ ○   2

0 ○ ○ ○   3

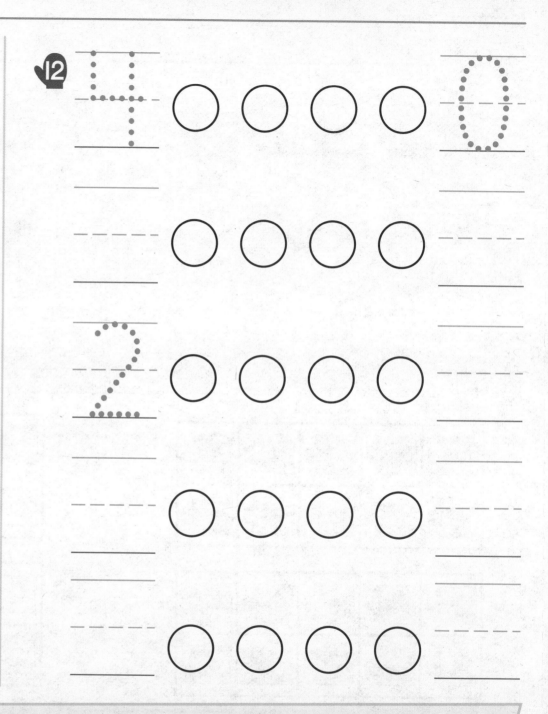

Directions 🪭 Have students use two different colored crayons to complete the pattern showing all of the ways to make 4, and then write the numbers.

Name _____

☆ 1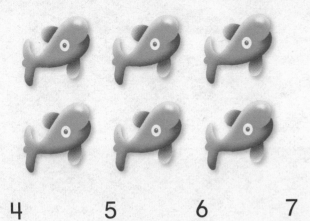

4   5   6   7
Ⓐ   Ⓑ   Ⓒ   Ⓓ

🍎 2

7   8   9   10
Ⓐ   Ⓑ   Ⓒ   Ⓓ

⭐ 3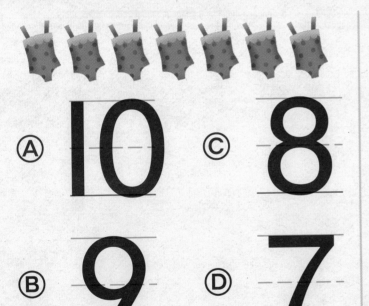

Ⓐ **10**   Ⓒ **8**

Ⓑ **9**   Ⓓ **7**

💜 4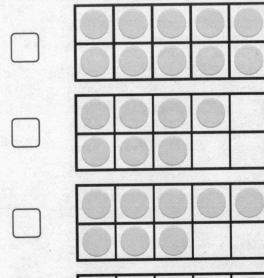

Directions Have students mark the best answer. ☆ How many fish are there? 🍎 How many turtles are there? ⭐ Which number tells how many swimsuits? 💜 Mark all the answers that do NOT show 9.

8

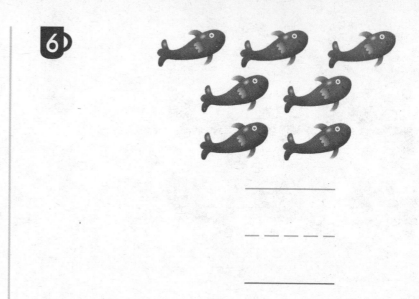

_____

- - - - - -

_____

_____

- - - - - -

_____

Topic 3 | Assessment

Name _____

8

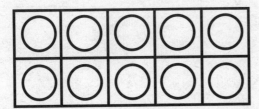

_____ _____

- - - - - - - - - -

_____ and _____

9

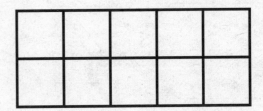

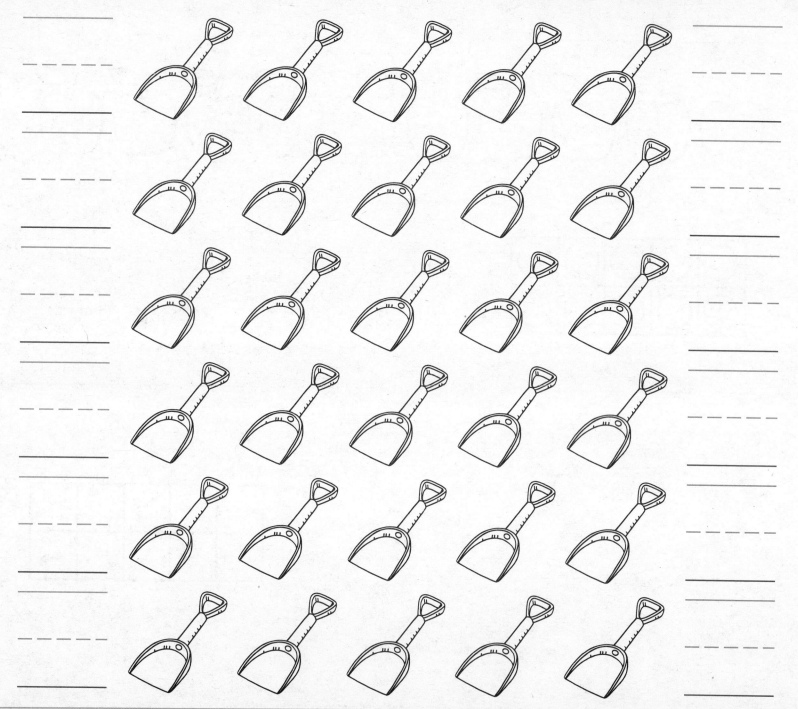

Name _____

⭐ 1

🐚 _____

⭐ _____

🦅 _____

🍎 2

_____   _____

- - - - -   - - - - -

- - - - -   - - - - -

_____   _____

Directions **The Beach** Say: *Lexi sees many interesting things at the beach.* ⭐ Have students count how many there are of each object, and then write the number to tell how many. 🍎 The fish that Lexi sees show one way to make 10. Color the fish red and yellow to show two different ways to make 10. Then write the numbers.

Topic 3 | Performance Assessment

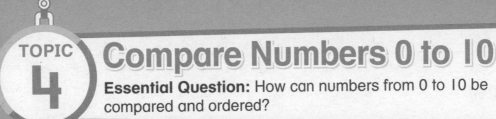

TOPIC 4

Compare Numbers 0 to 10

Essential Question: How can numbers from 0 to 10 be compared and ordered?

Digital Resources

Solve   Learn   Glossary

Tools   Assessment   Help   Games

Math and Science Project: Weather Changes

Directions Read the character speech bubbles to students. **Find Out!** Have students find out about weather changes. Say: *The weather changes from day to day. Talk to friends and relatives about the weather. Ask them to help you record the number of sunny days and rainy days during the week.*
Journal: Make a Poster Have students make a poster. Have them draw up to 10 lightning bolts above one house and up to 10 lightning bolts above another house. Ask them to write the number of lightning bolts above each house, and then draw a circle around the number that is greater than the other, or draw a circle around both numbers if they are the same.

Name _____

Review What You Know

1

2

3

4

_____

_ _ _ _ _

_____

5

_____

_ _ _ _ _

6

_____

_ _ _ _ _

Directions Have students: **1** draw a circle around the group of birds that is less than the other group; **2** draw a circle around the group of dogs that is greater than the other group; **3** draw a circle around the two groups that have an equal number of marbles; **4–6** count the number of objects, and then write the number to tell how many.

200 two hundred

Topic 4

Directions Say: *Emily visits a chicken farm. She sees a group of black chicks and a group of yellow chicks. Does Emily see more black or yellow chicks? How do you know?*

I can ... compare groups of up to 10 objects.

I can also reason about math.

☆ Guided Practice

★
1

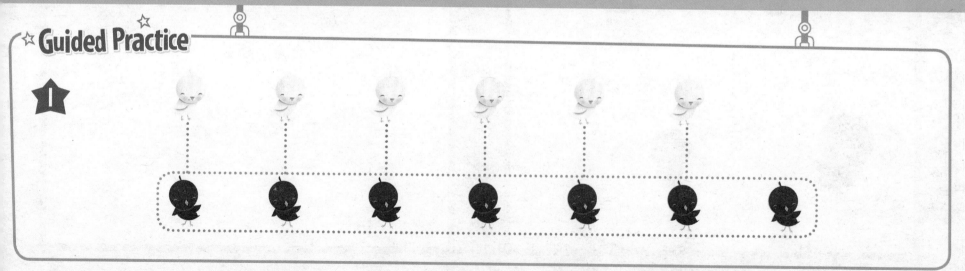

Directions ★ Have students compare the groups, draw a line from each chick in the top group to a chick in the bottom group, and then draw a circle around the group that is greater in number than the other group.

202 two hundred two

Copyright © Savvas Learning Company LLC. All Rights Reserved.

Topic 4 | Lesson I

Name _____

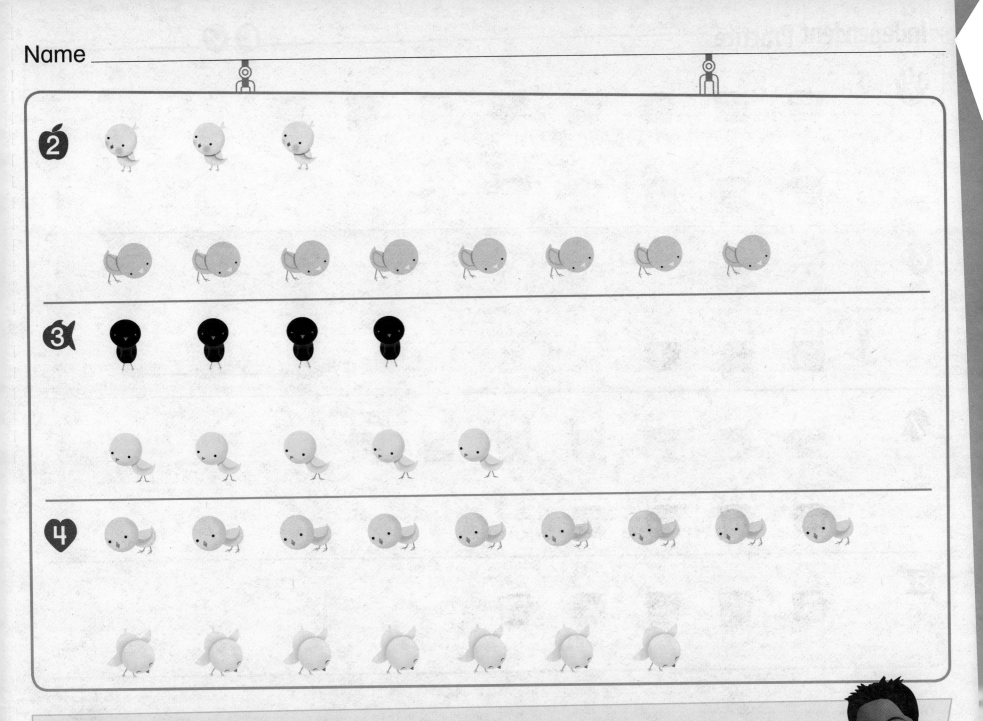

2

3

4

Directions ❷ **Math and Science** Say: *Chicks live in coops. Coops protect chicks in different types of weather.* Have students compare the groups, draw a line from each chick in the top group to a chick in the bottom group, and then draw a circle around the group that is greater in number than the other group. ❸ and ❹ Have students compare the groups, draw a line from each chick in the top group to a chick in the bottom group, and then draw a circle around the group that is less in number than the other group.

Independent Practice

Tools Assessment

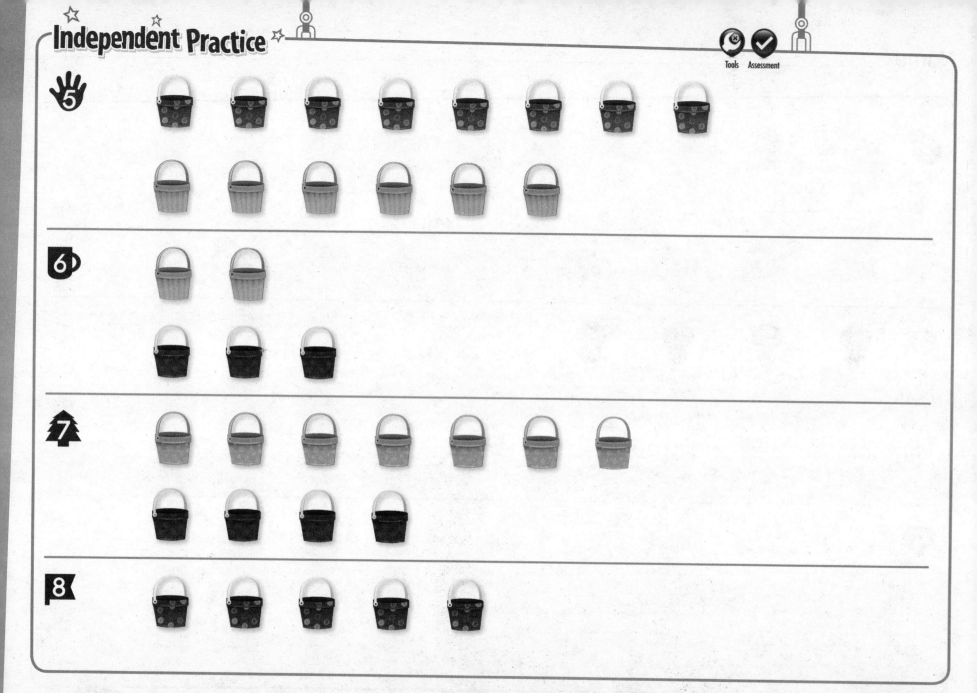

Directions Have students: ✋ compare the groups, draw a line from each bucket in the top group to a bucket in the bottom group, and then draw a circle around the group that is greater in number than the other group; ⑥ and ⑦ compare the groups, draw a line from each bucket in the top group to a bucket in the bottom group, and then draw a circle around the group that is less in number than the other group. ⑧ **Higher Order Thinking** Have students draw a group of buckets that is greater in number than the group shown.

204 two hundred four

Copyright © Savvas Learning Company LLC. All Rights Reserved.

Topic 4 | Lesson 1

Name _____

Another Look!

HOME ACTIVITY Draw a group of up to 9 dots. Ask your child to draw a group that has more dots than the group of dots you drew. Then have your child draw a group that has fewer dots than the group of dots you drew.

Directions Say: *Compare the groups. Draw a circle around the group of counters that is greater in number than the other.* Have students: ⭐ compare the groups and draw a circle around the group of counters that is greater in number than the other group; ② and ③ compare the groups and draw a circle around the group of counters that is less in number than the other group.

4

5

6

7

Topic 4 | Lesson 1

Solve & Share

Name _____

Solve

- - - - -

- - - - -

Directions Say: *Emily is planting seedlings, or little plants. She plants 5 red pepper seedlings and 7 yellow pepper seedlings. Use counters to show the groups of seedlings. Write the numbers, and then circle the number that tells which group has more.*

I can ...
compare groups of numbers using numerals to 10.

I can also make sense of problems.

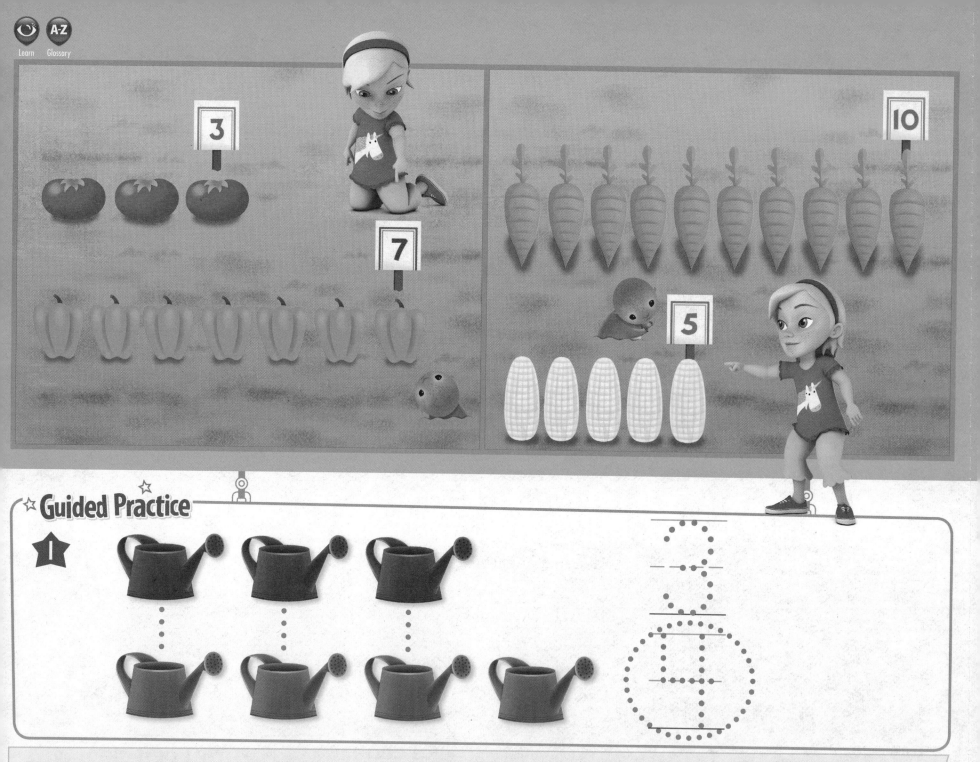

☆ Guided Practice

1

Directions 🌟 Have students count the watering cans in each group, write the number to tell how many, draw a line from each watering can in the top group to a watering can in the bottom group, and then draw a circle around the number that is greater than the other number.

Topic 4 | **Lesson 2**

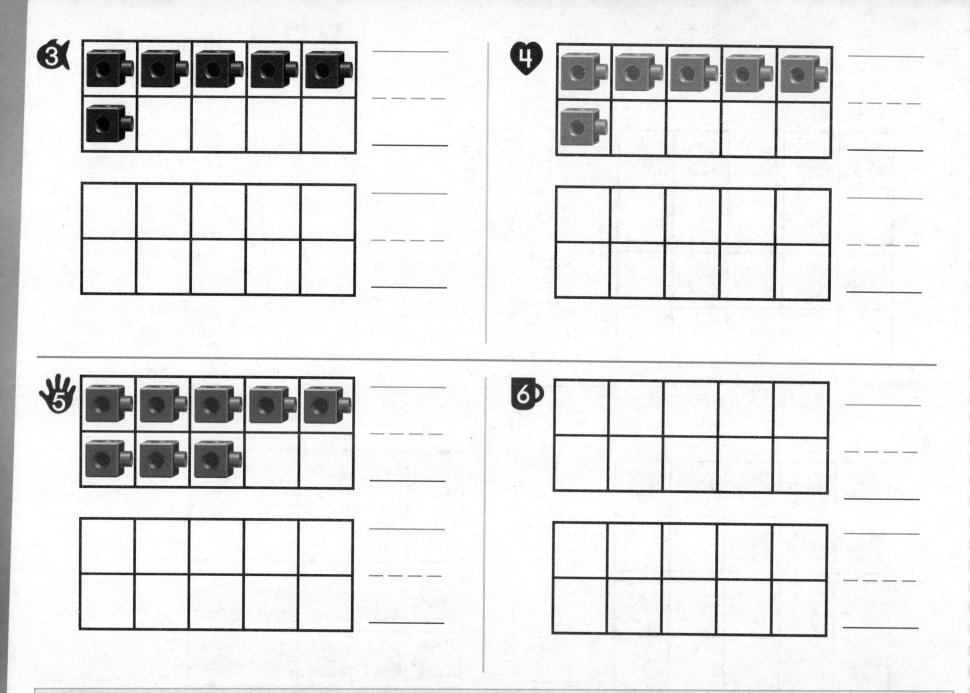

Directions Have students: ❸ count the cubes, draw a group of cubes that is less in number than the number of cubes counted, and then write the number to tell how many; ❹ and ❺ count the cubes, draw a group of cubes that is greater in number than the number of cubes counted, and then write the numbers to tell how many. ❻ **Higher Order Thinking** Have students draw a group of cubes in the top ten-frame, then in the bottom ten-frame draw a group of cubes that is equal in number to the first group they drew, and then write the numbers to tell how many.

Solve & Share

Name _____

Solve

Directions Say: *The class aquarium has two kinds of fish, goldfish and tetras. Write numbers to tell how many of each kind. Draw a circle around the fish that has a number greater than the other. Show how you know you are right.*

I can ... compare groups of numbers by counting.

I can also be precise in my work.

8

6

1 2 3 4 5 ⑥ 7 ⑧ 9 10

☆ Guided Practice

1 2 3 4 5 6 7 8 9 10

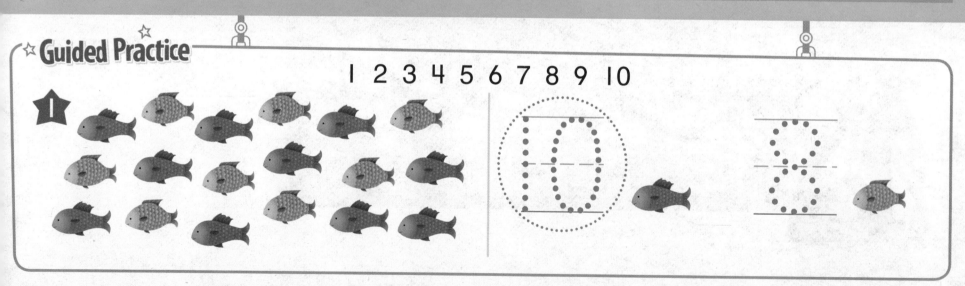

Topic 4 | Lesson 3

Name _____

1 2 3 4 5 6 7 8 9 10

2

3

4

5

Directions **Math and Science** Say: *Fish keep warm in extreme cold by staying deep in the water.* Have students count the number of each color fish, write the numbers to tell how many, and then: 2 draw a circle around the number that is greater than the other number; 3 draw a circle around both numbers if they are equal, or mark an X on both numbers if they are NOT equal; 4 and 5 mark an X on the number that is less than the other number. Use the number sequence to help find the answer for each problem.

1 2 3 4 5 6 7 8 9 10

Tools Assessment

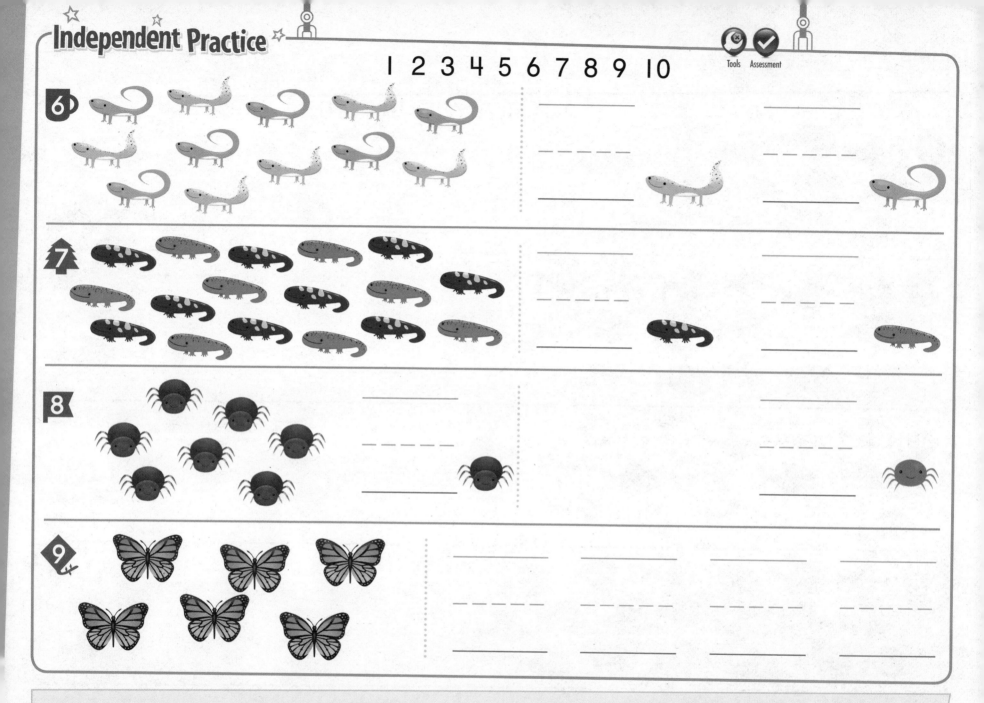

Directions Have students count the number of each critter, write the numbers to tell how many, and then: 🎁 draw a circle around both numbers if they are equal, or mark an X on both numbers if they are NOT equal; 🌲 mark an X on the number that is less than the other number; 🚩 draw a group of spiders that is two greater in number than the number of tarantulas shown, and then write the number to tell how many. 🔶 **Higher Order Thinking** Have students count the butterflies, and then write all the numbers up to 10 that are greater than the number of butterflies shown. Use the number sequence to help find the answer for each problem.

Topic 4 | **Lesson 3**

Name _____

Compare Groups to 10 by Counting

Another Look!

1 2 3 4 5 6 7 8 9 10

HOME ACTIVITY Shake up to 10 pennies and up to 10 nickels in your hand. Let them fall in a random group on the table. Have your child count the number of each coin, write the numbers, and then hold up the coin of the number that is greater. Repeat with different numbers of coins. Vary the activity by also asking them to hold up the coin of the number that is less, or hold up both if the numbers are equal.

1 2 3 4 5 6 7 8 9 10

⭐1

_____

- - - - - - - - - -

_____

Directions Say: *Count the red cubes. Then count the blue cubes. Write the numbers to tell how many of each color. Draw a circle around the number that is greater than the other number. Count the numbers 1 to 10 and use the number sequence to help find the answer.*
⭐ Have students count the number of each color cube, write the numbers to tell how many, and then draw a circle around the number that is greater than the other number. Use the number sequence to help find the answer.

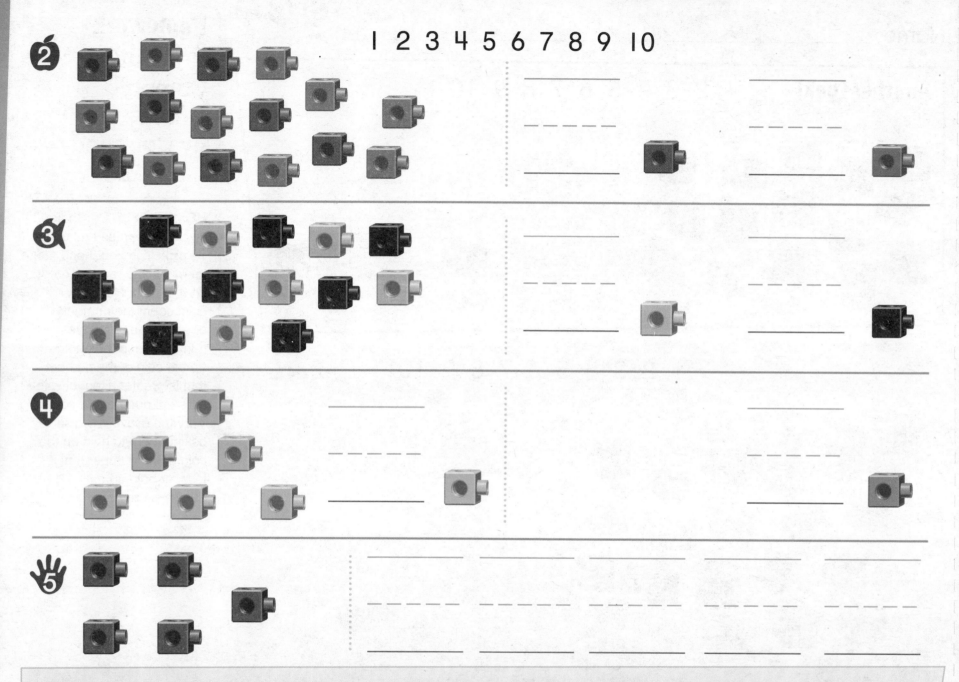

1 2 3 4 5 6 7 8 9 10

Directions Have students count the number of each color cube, write the numbers to tell how many, and then: ② mark an X on the number that is less than the other number; ③ draw a circle around both numbers if they are equal, or mark an X on both numbers if they are NOT equal. ④ Have students draw a group of blue cubes that is equal to the number of cubes shown. ⑤ **Higher Order Thinking** Have students count the cubes, and then write all the numbers that are greater than the number of cubes shown up to 10. Use the number sequence to help find the answer for each problem.

Solve & Share

Name _____

Solve

1 2 3 4 5 6 7 8 9 10

Directions Say: Emily's mother asked her to bring the towels in off the line. Her basket can hold less than 7 towels. How many towels might Emily bring in? You can give more than one answer. Show how you know your answers are right.

I can ... compare two numbers.

I can also model with math.

Topic 4 | Lesson 4
Digital Resources at SavvasRealize.com
two hundred nineteen **219**

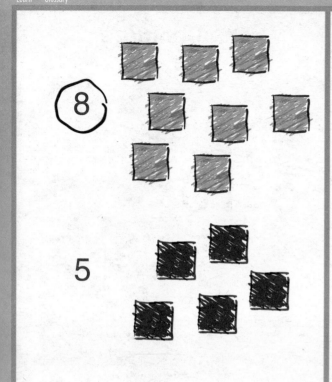

⑧

5

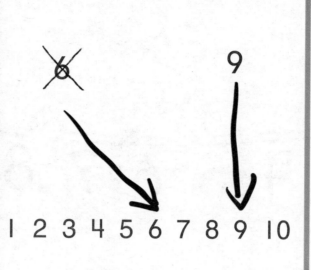

~~6~~   9

1 2 3 4 5 6 7 8 9 10

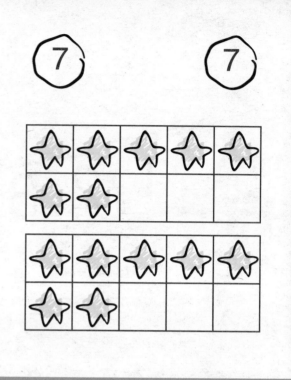

⑦   ⑦

☆ Guided Practice

⭐ **1**

7   ⦙8⦙

1 2 3 4 5 6 7 8 9 10

🍎 **2**   6

4

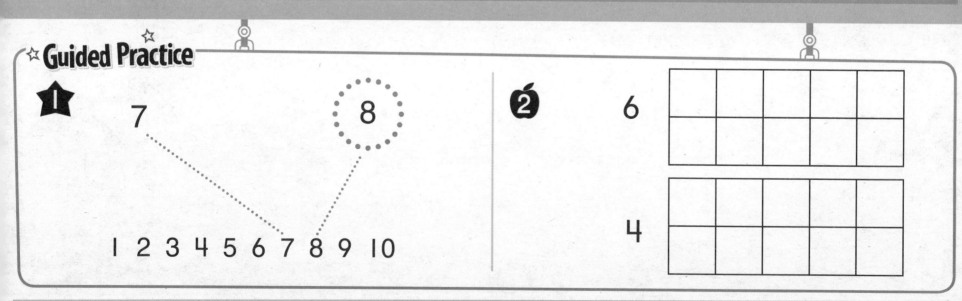

Directions Have students: ⭐ count the numbers 1 to 10 and use the number sequence to show how they know which number is greater than the other, and then draw a circle around the number that is greater; 🍎 draw counters in the ten-frames to show how they know which number is greater than the other, and then draw a circle around the number that is greater.

Name _____

❸

6

9

♥

8

8

✋

9   10

1 2 3 4 5 6 7 8 9 10

☕

9

8

Directions Have students: ❸ draw pictures to show how they know which number is greater than the other, and then draw a circle around the number that is greater; ♥ draw counters in the ten-frames to show how they know if the numbers are equal, and then draw a circle around both numbers if they are equal, or mark an X on both numbers if they are NOT equal; ✋ use the number sequence to show how they know which number is less than the other number, and then mark an X on the number that is less; ☕ draw pictures to show how they know which number is less than the other number, and then mark an X on the number that is less.

Tools Assessment

7

6

8

8

9   7

1 2 3 4 5 6 7 8 9 10

9

8   _ _ _ _ _ _   _ _ _ _ _ _

10

5   _ _ _ _ _   9

Directions Have students: **7** draw pictures to show how they know which number is less than the other number, and then mark an X on the number that is less; **8** use the number sequence to show how they know which number is less than the other number, and then mark an X on the number that is less. **9** **Higher Order Thinking** Have students write the next two numbers that are greater than the number shown, and then tell how they know. **10** **Higher Order Thinking** Have students write a number that is greater than the number on the left, but less than the number on the right.

Topic 4 | Lesson 4

Name _____

Homework
& Practice 4-4
Compare
Numbers to 10

Another Look!

9

7

HOME ACTIVITY Give your child 10 pennies and 10 nickels. Write two numbers on a sheet of paper and ask your child to show the two numbers using the coins. Then have your child draw a circle around the number that is greater, mark an X on the number that is less, or draw a circle around both numbers if they are equal.

⭐1

6

7

🍎2

8

6

Directions Say: *Draw counters in the ten-frames to help find the answer. Then compare the numbers and draw a circle around the number that is greater than the other number.* Have students draw counters in the ten-frames to help find the answer, and then: ⭐ draw a circle around the number that is greater than the other number; 🍎 mark an X on the number that is less than the other number.

Topic 4 | Lesson 4   Digital Resources at SavvasRealize.com   two hundred twenty-three **223**

❸

5

[ten-frame]

7

[ten-frame]

❹

8

8

✋5

8

_____

- - - - - - -

_____

[ten-frame]

[ten-frame]

☕6

_____

- - - - - - -

_____

Solve

_____
- - - - -
_____

8

_____
- - - - -
_____

Directions Say: *Emily thinks of two numbers, one that is 1 less than 8 and another that is 1 more than 8. Write the two numbers Emily is thinking of. Show how you know you are correct.*

I can ...
count groups of numbers to 10.

I can also reason about math.

Digital Resources at SavvasRealize.com

0 1 2   3 4 5   6 7 8   9 10

☆ Guided Practice

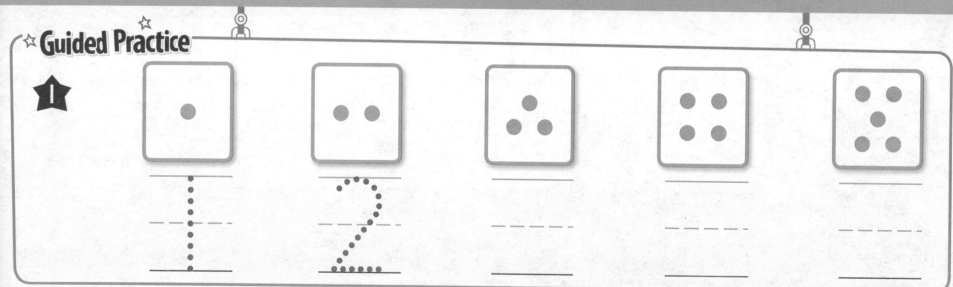

★1

Directions ★1 Have students count, and then write the number that is 1 greater than the number before.

Name _____

2

_____ **7** _____

3

6	9
8	7

_____ _____ _____ _____

_____ _____ _____ _____

4

3	6
5	4

_____ _____ _____ _____

_____ _____ _____ _____

Directions ❷ **Vocabulary** Have students count to find the number that is 1 **less than** and 1 **greater than** the given number, and then write the numbers. ❸ and ❹ Have students write the smallest number, and then count forward and write the number that is 1 greater than the number before.

Tools Assessment

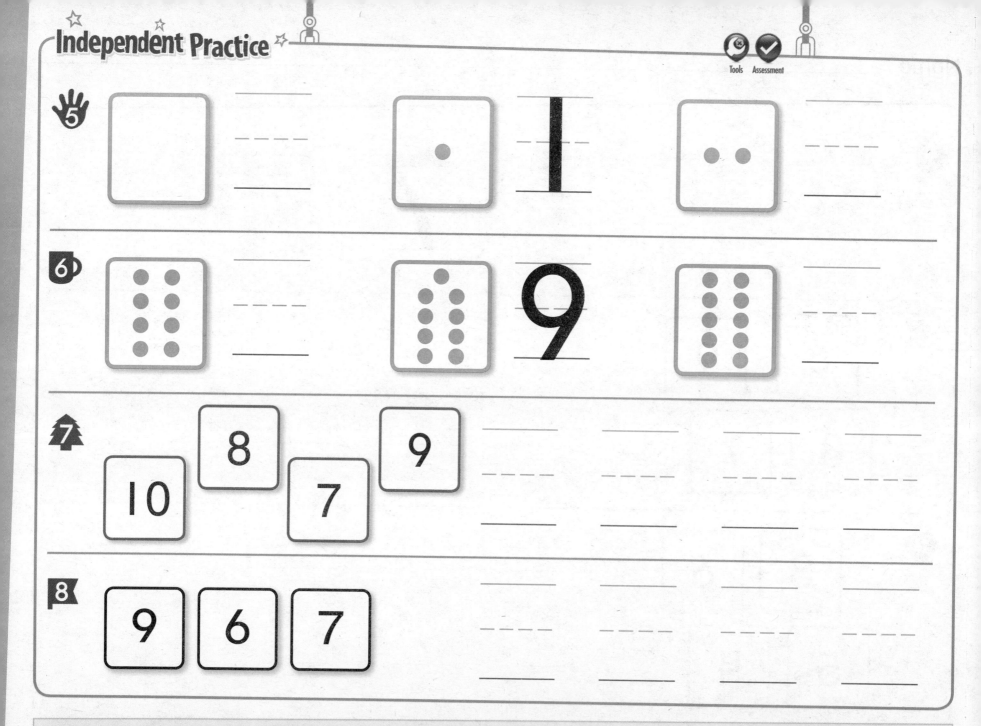

5

6

7

8

Directions Have students: 👋 and 🐥 count to find the number that is 1 less than and 1 greater than the given number, and then write the numbers; 🌲 compare the number cards, write the smallest number, and then count forward and write the number that is 1 greater than the number before. 🏴 **Higher Order Thinking** Have students find the missing number, and then count forward to write the number that is 1 greater than the number before.

Name _____

Another Look!

0 1 2

⭐ 1

6

② 2

5

③ 3

❤ 4

Directions Say: *Write the numbers that are 1 less than and 1 greater than 1. Count the numbers aloud.* Then have students: ⭐ and ② count to find the number that is 1 less than and 1 greater than the given number, and then write the numbers; ③ and ❤ compare the number cards, write the smallest number, and then count forward and write the number that is 1 greater than the number before.

5

6

7 | 6 | 3 | 5 |

8

Solve & Share

Solve

Think.

_____

_ _ _ _ _ _

_____

Directions Say: *There are 7 fish in a bowl. Emily puts 1 more fish in the bowl. How many fish are in the bowl now? How can you solve this problem?*

I can ...
repeat something from one problem to help me solve another problem.

I can also compare numbers to 10.

Learn   Glossary

☆ Guided Practice

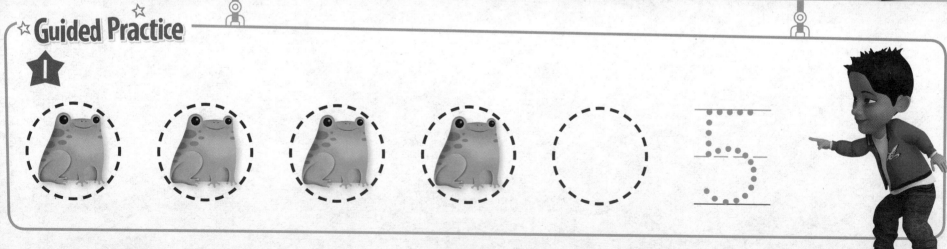

Directions ⭐ Say: *Carlos sees 4 frogs at the pond. Then he sees 1 more. How many frogs are there now?* Have students use reasoning to find the number that is 1 greater than the number of frogs shown. Draw counters to show the answer, and then write the number. Have students explain their reasoning.

Tools   Assessment

Independent Practice

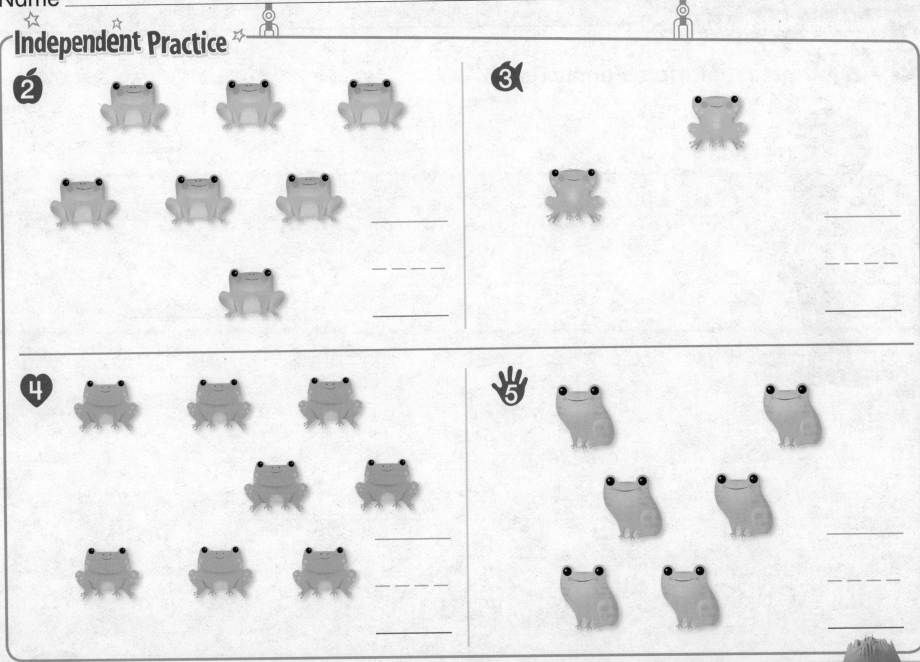

2 (frogs) _____

3 (frogs) - - - -

4 (frogs) - - - -

5 (frogs) - - - -

Directions Say: *Alex sees frogs at the pond. Then he sees 1 more. How many frogs are there now?* **2–5** Have students use reasoning to find the number that is 1 greater than the number of frogs shown. Draw counters to show the answer, and then write the number. Have students explain their reasoning.

Marta's Family Pets

· ·

_____

- - - -

_____

Name _____

Another Look!

HOME ACTIVITY Give your child 10 crayons. Then place a row of 8 paper clips, or other small objects, on a table. Ask your child to make a row of crayons that is 1 greater in number than the number of paper clips and then tell how many. Repeat with other numbers.

- - - - -

_____

- - - - -

_____

- - - - -

_____

Directions Say: *You can show 1 more than the group of butterflies using counters. Use reasoning to find the number that is 1 greater than the number of butterflies shown. Draw counters to show your answer, and then write the number.* Have students explain their reasoning. Have students: 🌟 and 🍎 *use reasoning to find the number that is 1 greater than the spiders or butterflies shown. Draw counters to show the answer, and then write the number;* 🐟 *use counters to find the number that is 2 greater than the number of spiders shown, draw the counters, and then write the number.* Have students explain their reasoning.

Comparing Goldfish

. . . .

. . . .

Directions   Read the problem aloud. Then have students use multiple problem-solving methods to solve the problem. Say: *Alex has 7 goldfish. Marta has 1 more goldfish than Alex. Emily has 1 more goldfish than Marta. How many goldfish does Emily have?* 🖤 **Generalize** *What part of the problem repeats? How does that help to solve the problem?* ✋ **Use Tools** *What tool can you use to help solve the problem? Use the tool to find the number of goldfish Emily has.* 🖤 **Make Sense** *Which person should have a number of goldfish greater than the others? How do you know?*

1

6   9

2

_____

- - - - - - - - - -

_____

3

_____

- - - - - - - - - -

_____

4

_____

- - - - - - - - - -

_____

Directions   Understand Vocabulary Have students: **1** draw a circle around the number that is **greater than** 7; **2** **count** the counters, and then write the number to tell how many; **3** write the number that means **none**; **4** count how many of each color cube there is, draw a circle around the group that has a number of cubes that is **less than** the other group, and then write the number to tell how many there are in that group.

5

3   8

6

_____
- - - - - -
_____

7

_____
- - - - - -
_____

8

_____
5 - - - - - - 9
_____

Set A

⭐ 1

Set B

⑥

② 🍎

4

Directions Have students: ⭐ compare the groups, and draw a circle around the group that is less in number than the other group; ② count the fruit in each group, write the numbers that tell how many, draw a line from each piece of fruit in the top group to a piece of fruit in the bottom group, and then draw a circle around the number that is greater than the other number.

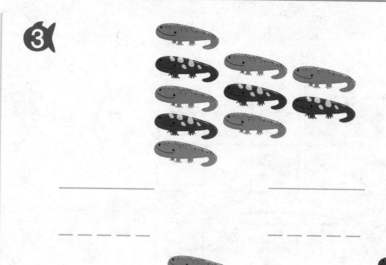

5

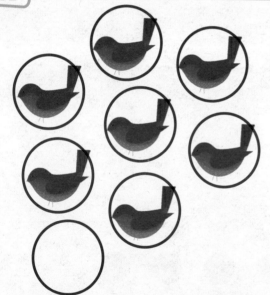

8

Directions Have students: ❸ count the number of each critter, write the numbers, and then mark an X on the number that is less than the other number; ❹ Say: *April sees frogs at the pond. Then she sees 1 more. How many frogs does she see now?* Have students use reasoning to find the number that is 1 greater than the number of frogs shown. Draw counters to show the answer, and then write the number.

Name _____

⭐ 1

Ⓐ

Ⓑ

Ⓒ

Ⓓ

🍎 2

7

☐ 9

☐ 6

☐ 5

☐ 3

🐦 3

_____ _____

- - - - - - -   - - - - - -

_____   _____

Directions Have students mark the best answer. ⭐ Which group of blue birds is greater in number than the group of yellow birds? 🍎 Mark all the numbers that are less than the number on the card. 🐦 Have students count the number of lemons and limes, write the number that tells how many of each, and then draw a circle around the number that is greater.

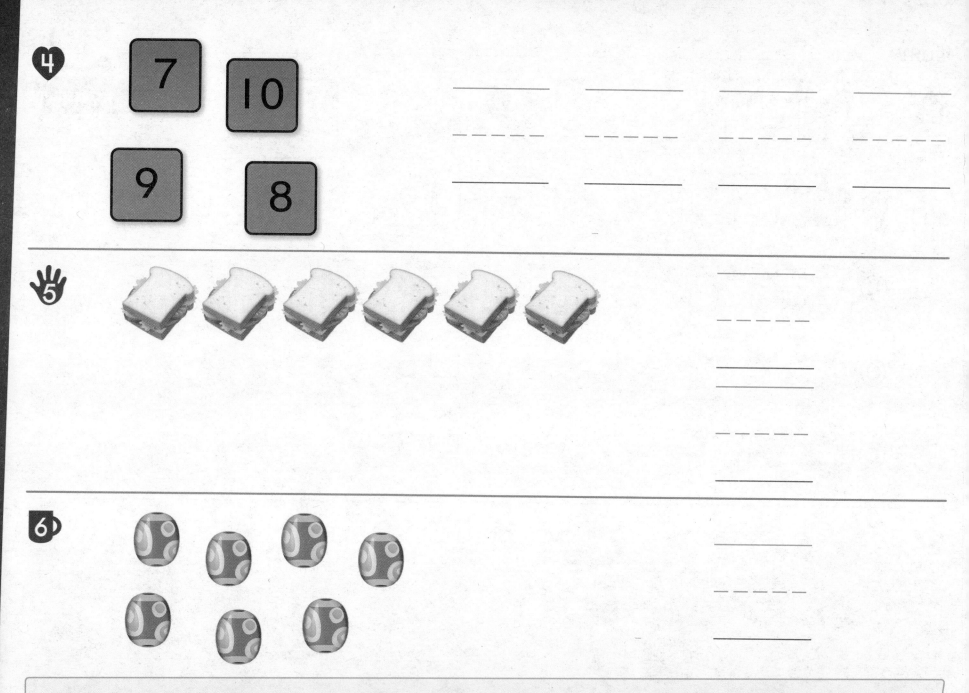

♥ 4

7   10

9   8

✋ 5

☕ 6

Directions Have students: ♥ write the smallest number, and then count forward and write the number that is 1 greater than the number before; ✋ count the sandwiches in the group, draw a group of juice boxes that is less in number than the group of sandwiches shown, and then write the numbers to tell how many. ☕ Say: *Kayla has 7 beads to make a bracelet. Then she buys 1 more. How many beads does she have now?* Have students use reasoning to find the number that is 1 greater than the number of beads shown. Draw counters to show the answer, and then write the number to tell how many.

Name _____

1 2 3 4 5 6 7 8 9 10

_____   _____

- - - -

_____

Directions **Forest Animals** Say: *The forest is home to woodland animals. One part of the forest has many different animal homes in it.*
★ Have students study the picture. Say: *How many skunks live in this part of the forest? How many raccoons live in this part of the forest? Count the number of each type of animal and write the numbers.* Then have students draw a circle around the number that is greater than the other number and mark an X on the number that is less than the other number. Have them use the number sequence to help find the answers.

Topic 4 | Performance Assessment   two hundred forty-three **243**

2

_____ _____ _____ _____

_____

3

5

5

4

- - - - -   - - - - -

_____   _____